Rich by Thirty

Rich by Thirty

A YOUNG ADULT'S GUIDE TO FINANCIAL SUCCESS

LESLEY SCORGIE

KEY PORTER BOOKS

Library and Archives Canada Cataloguing in Publication

Scorgie, Lesley

  Rich by thirty / Lesley Scorgie.

ISBN-13: 978-1-55263-794-4

1. Young adults—Finance, Personal. 2. Teenagers—Finance, Personal. I. Title.

HG179.S353 2006   332.0240084'2   C2006-903134-7

 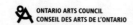

The publisher gratefully acknowledges the support of the Canada Council for the Arts and the Ontario Arts Council for its publishing program. We acknowledge the support of the Government of Ontario through the Ontario Media Development Corporation's Ontario Book Initiative.

We acknowledge the financial support of the Government of Canada through the Book Publishing Industry Development Program (BPIDP) for our publishing activities.

Key Porter Books Limited
Six Adelaide Street East, Tenth Floor
Toronto, Ontario
Canada M5C 1H6

www.keyporter.com

Text design: Martin Gould
Electronic formatting: Jean Lightfoot Peters

Printed and bound in Canada

07 08 09 10 11 5 4 3

To my Grandmother Scorgie. Words cannot express how much your love, care, and influence have meant to me throughout the years. You are the greatest woman I have ever met—full of strength, courage, intelligence, beauty and support. I am so blessed to have you in my life.

Acknowledgements

I would like to sincerely thank my family—Mom, Dad, Alison, and Stephen—for fuelling my life's ambitions with love and support. Thank you also to my extended family. You have cheered me on all the way to success. Thanks to my wonderful friends who have taught me how to love, to laugh, to cry, to be strong, and, best of all, to become me. Your inspiration and care over the years have been and will continue to be irreplaceable.

There are so many people that have taken time out of busy schedules to invest and nurture my professional development. I want to thank those individuals who have guided me in my career and passions. My Rich by Thirty website and newsletter team, Erin and Marco: thanks for your exceptional efforts. We are making a difference! Finally, I want to thank Key Porter Books and KMLA for making my dreams of becoming an author come true.

Contents

Introduction   11

1 Get Motivated:
   WHY MONEY MATTERS   19

2 Get Organized:
   FILE FOLDERS, BANKS, AND YOU   31

3 Get Started:
   THE JOYS OF BUDGETING   44

4 Get Out from Under:
   AVOIDING THE CREDIT CRUNCH   63

5 Get Saving:
   RIGHT HERE, RIGHT NOW   76

6   **Get Investing, Part I:**
THE BASICS   **90**

7   **Get Investing, Part II:**
OPTIONS AND STRATEGIES   **108**

8   **Get Specific:**
HOMES, KIDS, AND STUFF LIKE THAT   **136**

Conclusion   **152**

Index   **156**

Introduction

A few years ago, I met a woman whose story has stayed with me to this day. In fact, she's one of the reasons I decided to write this book. Mary was nearly seventy years old. She told me about the financial struggles and successes she'd experienced throughout her life. When she was young, she married and became pregnant. Her husband left her near the end of her pregnancy, taking the household savings with him. Mary was on her own—scared and expecting a new addition to her life.

Mary's son quickly became her reason to live and survive. Almost immediately after his birth, she had to find a job. After all, no one else was going to support them! With few family members or friends nearby, Mary relied on kind neighbours to look after the baby while she filed books at the local library. Her paycheques evaporated within days.

Mary learned how to live a frugal life. She planned and documented her spending so that she could provide for the needs of her small family. Only the basics were affordable.

There was no money left over for saving, trips, books, or entertainment. After a few years of living paycheque to paycheque Mary was feeling defeated. She felt she was getting nowhere. Yes, she and her son were surviving, but questions were flying through her head. How could she get ahead financially when she was barely making minimum wage? Would she ever be able to afford a home in a safe neighbourhood where her son could play outside? What about retirement? What would happen if her son wanted to go to college? What if she lost her job? Would she be able to pay the bills?

When the questions became too much to handle, Mary decided to take control. She borrowed money management books from the library, talked to friends and family, and saw a financial adviser for the first time. She worked out a long-term financial strategy that focused on saving what little she did have. It was the only way she would feel secure, she decided. It was the only solution she could find to her financial problems.

Mary was only twenty-three years old when she made that decision—the decision to take control of her financial life. When Mary retired at the age of sixty-five, she owned a modest home with no mortgage and a fuel-efficient vehicle. Her son had graduated from college with her help, and, better still, Mary had more than $650,000 in retirement savings!

Have you ever felt like Mary did in the early years with her son? Have you ever felt that saving money was something you'd never be able to do? Have you ever felt that you'll never get ahead? Have you ever wanted something so badly and yet not been able to afford it? We've all had these feelings! But, like Mary, you can take control of the situation and learn how to overcome your particular obstacles. Whether you're in a situation like Mary and her son, or whether you just want to put some money away for a rainy day, the financial fundamentals you'll find in this book will see you through to a very wealthy life—in more ways than one.

Why Listen to Me?

Before you read any further, you'd probably like to know a little more about me. Who am I, and why am I telling you how to manage your money? Good questions!

I was born in Toronto, Ontario, in 1983 into an average family. My mom stayed at home until I was four years old, and my dad worked as a paramedic. When I was eight, my family moved out west to Edmonton, Alberta, so that both of my parents could go back to school and upgrade their education. As you can imagine, with both of my parents in school, money was *very* tight. When they graduated in 1998, my family moved again—this time to Calgary so that my parents could look for work in their respective fields. For the next four years, my family struggled with job stability and finances.

I didn't grow up in a wealthy home. Far from it. There were years in the mid-nineties when my family survived on $24,000 a year. That managed to feed and clothe five people, pay a small mortgage, pay parental tuition, and maintain one vehicle. For more than ten years, we had very small Christmas gifts, generic brand food, and no lavish vacations. My brother, sister, and I relied on second-hand stores for our bicycles, clothing, and toys. There was no money to spare. It was during that time that I learned to live the frugal life. That meant my entire family would look for deals, sales, and giveaways. We never paid full price for anything!

It's not hard to figure out that my interest in money was sparked by the lack of it in my own home. Even at an early age, I'd carry around my piggy bank and inquire about the different coins that I'd collected and what I could purchase with them. My parents kindly answered most of my money questions, even though they were drowning in debt and bills. They also encouraged me to read up on my interest. Soon, I began to flip through *Forbes* and *Report on Business*. I picked my way through various articles and understood at least some of what I read. While I was reading about stock picking and entrepreneurial endeavours, my best friends were watching *Mighty Power Rangers*. I joined them on occasion, but more times than not, I fell deeper into my own interests.

As early as eight, I was operating a lemonade stand during the summer months and shovelling snow during the winter. I wanted to earn enough money for a trip to the pool, a visit to the candy store, or an outing to a movie. I set my sights, knew my targets, and went for it. As time passed, my initial motivations for saving and investing evolved from "making enough to go to the movies" to "making enough to retire with millions."

On my tenth birthday, with $100 of gift money, I purchased my first Canada Savings Bond. My mom believed it was a great idea for me to learn first-hand what investing money was all about. From that time on, I took every chance I could get to buy more bonds.

When I turned fourteen, I started working at the local public library. Not only did it earn me a small income, it gave me the chance to learn more about growing money through the books and newspapers I found on the shelves. I took it upon myself to investigate options for investing my money. I bought my first mutual funds that same year, and began investing in the stock market four years later, when I was eighteen. Once I started to see the growth in my own accounts—the power of compound interest—I was hooked!

From Frugal to Extraordinary: The Oprah Experience

In grade eleven, my management and marketing class was learning about investing. My teacher was having difficulty explaining the concept to our class because my peers were totally unresponsive. One day, in complete frustration, she asked if any student would like to try teaching this part of the course. I raised my hand and away we went.

I took a few class periods to share my knowledge with my friends. It just so happened that, during the same week, a local newspaper phoned the school to ask if there were any "odd or interesting" students they could profile. I was nominated due to my financial knowledge. The newspaper agreed that I fit the criteria—I hoped I was more interesting than odd!—and they went ahead with the interview. They published a front-page article entitled "Whiz Kid" and then posted it on the Internet.

In February 2001, I received a phone call from a producer at the *Oprah Winfrey Show*. She had seen the article on the Internet and wanted to talk about my investment and money management savvy. Two weeks later, I was on the show!

The theme was "Ordinary People, Extraordinary Wealth." I was one of a few guests that were sharing their financial savvy and secrets with more than twenty million viewers! What set me apart from the others? I was the only guest under the age of forty. I was there to demonstrate that you can have a very typical young life and still make positive financial choices.

Since being on *Oprah*, I have completed my bachelor of commerce degree and written for a number of newspapers and magazines. I am now twenty-three years old. I own a house, have a good job, and savings for the future. I also have a lot of fun! By the time I retire, I'll have millions of dollars in savings and assets. Because of this success, I've become a spokesperson and advocate for young people who want to chase their dreams and be fully equipped to handle the price tag. My passion is for teaching and speaking about money management and financial literacy. I have delivered presentations to thousands of people across North America, with audiences ranging in age from six to eighty.

Before we go any further, I want to assure you that I was (and still am!) *normal*—like you! I went to school, worked a part-time job through high school and university, and completed my homework even when it was tough or boring. On weekends, I socialized with friends and squeezed in a little relaxing time. I went through the same ups and downs that every young person experiences. The only difference? I wanted to be wealthy by the time I was thirty and I started planning earlier than usual to make that happen.

Listen Up!

Out of all the advice you'll read in the pages that follow, this could be the most important: "normal" lives can lead to extraordinary accomplishments. You may think that you can't do this, or that what little you have to contribute to your own financial future isn't enough. You can, and it is. All of your time, talent, money, and effort will pay off in the long run if you can focus on making some positive choices. My own financial choices have led me to a point where I will have millions of dollars upon retirement. And the best part is that I haven't had to make huge sacrifices to get there.

So how do you do it? This book is going to get you started. As you read, you will find useful information on getting motivated and organized, getting smart with your money, and getting started with your savings and investing. Perhaps for the first time in your life, you'll be getting financial advice from someone your own age—someone like you. You'll learn basic money management, including how to make or find money, debt reduction, budgeting, and investment strategies. You'll learn how to live a frugal life without making painstaking sacrifices. You'll learn why it makes so much sense to start planning when you're young, and why it pays to diversify. You'll learn the difference between savings and investing, and pick up some short- and long-term investing strategies. Perhaps most importantly, you'll learn that money is only one part of a balanced and happy life.

When the tips, techniques, and strategies on the pages that follow are combined, they make for a very rich lifestyle and great personal and financial fulfillment. This book doesn't offer a "get rich quick" scheme. It is about learning the financial fundamentals that will secure your financial future in the long term. And by reading it, you are well on your way to financial success.

1

Get Motivated:

WHY MONEY MATTERS

It's not all about the money. At least that's what study results are telling us. These days, North Americans under thirty don't care about money nearly as much as previous generations did. These days, we're looking for balance and personal fulfillment. We seek opportunities for growth, flexibility, and fun in our professional and personal lives. And we're well aware that money doesn't necessarily provide all of the above.

On the one hand, I think it is fantastic that our generation is willing to separate the pursuit of happiness from that of monetary success. On the other, I truly believe that not caring about money is a big mistake! Being smart about your money—how you spend it, how you manage it—can make a huge difference to the quality of your life. It can open doors, or close them. It can help you realize your goals and dreams, or ensure that you won't.

A Few Boring Truths

Whether you want to face it or not, the future is upon you. Before you even know it, you'll be thinking about things like the cost of post-secondary education, mortgages, cars, kids, vacations, and—yup—retirement! It may sound boring, but it's your responsibility to think about these things. You must take positive steps now so that you can create the future that you want. You are the only one that can make your own dreams—financial and otherwise—come true. If you're not looking out for your future, who else will?

The Sort of Boring Truth about the Distant Future

Kevin is twenty-three years old, and the youngest of three children in his family. His mom and dad are both in their mid-sixties, but neither one can afford to retire. The situation is starting to worry Kevin. His parents seem tired all the time, and he's concerned about their health. He's even started to take on extra shifts at work so that he can help out with the bills and the groceries. One thing Kevin knows for sure is that he doesn't want to end up in the same position when he turns sixty! He knows that the only way to avoid this scenario is to work hard now and to get smart with his money.

Money is the key to your long-term financial security. It's scary to think about this, but by the time you're ready to retire, you will need approximately four times the amount of money that you need now—just to live the way that you're living now (keep those "lifestyles of the rich and famous" fantasies in check!). This hard-to-swallow truth is due to a nasty little thing called **inflation**. Inflation makes the dollars in your bank account today less powerful as time goes by. For example, $4 today might only be worth $1 forty years from now.

Think about it this way: a sixty-five-year-old woman with $1,000,000 in retirement savings could call it quits tomorrow and not have to live below the poverty line. However, forty years from now, a sixty-five-year-old woman wanting to call it quits would need to have socked away $4,000,000 to maintain her lifestyle! Another way to look at it is $1,000,000 today will be worth only $250,000 (approximately) in forty years.

If this isn't scary or depressing enough, wait until you hear the next part! The next time you receive a paycheque, have a look at the section on the stub where the deductions are listed. There are tax deductions and Canada Pension Plan (CPP) deductions and maybe others, too, like a health plan, or long-term disability. Let's focus on that CPP deduction. The government takes this money out of your pay and places it into a national fund that is supposed to help you when you retire. Great theory, right? Sure. The only problem is that, thanks to the huge number of baby boomer retirees, the government won't be of much help.

The bottom line is that while we might be able to count on the government for a little help with our retirement savings, we'll more likely have to count on ourselves. Boring, and a little bit depressing, but true.

So, your money becomes less and less powerful and valuable as time passes. And you're not likely to get much help from the government or anyone else, for that matter. Are you ever going to be able to retire? Or buy a house? Or go on vacation? Of course you will—if you learn to care about your money. Handled properly and managed wisely, your money can not only keep up with inflation, it can beat it!

The Not-So-Boring Truth about the Not-So-Distant Future

Maya is sixteen years old and in her second-last year of high school. She has average grades and comes from a financially average household. She loves to hang out with her friends, dance, and most importantly—shop!

Recently, Maya's started to think about what she might want to do with her life. She made an appointment with the guidance counsellor at school to discuss her dream of becoming a doctor. When she sat down with the counsellor, however, she discovered that the cost of medical school was huge *and that her grades would have to be* huge *as well if she had any chance of getting a scholarship. Now, Maya's reconsidering. Unless something changes—both with her commitment to school and her financial planning—her dream will never become a reality.*

If you were drifting off during the last section—or at least wondering why you need to think about retirement when you're still in your teens or twenties—maybe this section will hit home a little harder. You need to care about your money because, even though you're young, money still affects you. In fact, money affects everyone.

What do you want to do with your life? Do you want to be a pilot? A nurse? A musician? You'll need money to do it. Money is also necessary if you want to go snowboarding, buy a home, travel, or shop.

It comes down to this: money enables us to have choices. The more we understand about it—how to make it, how to save and invest it, how to spend it wisely—the more freedom we'll have. Think about how dull your life would be if you didn't have enough money to go to a movie with a friend. Think about how frustrated you would be if you really wanted to become a doctor, but couldn't afford the tuition fees. The more financial freedom you have, the more freedom you'll have in all areas of your life. You'll be free to make the choices that best suit your needs and goals. And isn't that what everyone wants?

THE $5,000 QUESTION

If you came home to find a cheque for $5,000 in your mailbox, what would you do with it? Would you save the money, buy a car, some clothes, or a hot new sound system? Would you give some to charity, pay off a loan, or take your friends out for a fabulous dinner? It's nice to have so many options, isn't it?

Now consider the opposite situation. Your most recent shopping trip got a little out of hand and you're looking at a $5,000 credit card bill! What are your options now? Remember, money leads to choices, and choices lead to freedom.

The Not-So-Boring Truth about Time

I know, I know. All this stuff about retirement and choices and freedom makes perfect sense to you, but still.... You're probably scratching your head right now, trying to figure out how you—an average under-thirty-year-old with hardly any disposable income—are supposed to take control of your financial life when some fifty- and sixty-year-olds haven't gotten the hang of it yet. They've got good jobs, and houses, and lots of other stuff that you don't, right? That's true. But you've got one thing that they don't have, and it may be the most important thing of all: time.

Time is a pretty handy thing to have on your side. With time, you can grow your money substantially without doing nearly as much work as you might expect. You can do this through the power of **compound interest**.

Imagine yourself at the top of a hill, making a snowball. It's a nice, round snowball that takes you all of thirty seconds to make. When you aren't looking, the wind blows the snowball down the hill. As it's rolling, it picks up more and more snow until, a couple of minutes later and with no additional help from you, a *giant* snowball lands at the bottom of the hill. That's how compound interest works. You earn interest on your initial investment, which is then reinvested, allowing you to earn interest on it as well. So now you're earning interest on your interest. As time passes, your growth "snowballs" into something quite impressive.

The chart on page 25 is an abbreviated version of one that you'll see later, in chapter 6. For now, all you need to know is that if you start early enough and contribute to an investment plan regularly—increasing your contribution levels as you advance in your life and career—you can turn yourself into a millionaire by starting with as little as $35 a month (these results are based on generating an 8.5 per cent return on your investments).

The Power of Compound Interest*

AGE	SAVED PER MONTH	TOTAL SAVED (WITH COMPOUND INTEREST)
16	$35	$455.70
23	$150	$6,432.82
30	$250	$30,384.16
40	$350	$118,288.33
65		$1,047,289.30

Impressive, isn't it? If the chart isn't enough to inspire you, think about it this way: you can actually double your money with the power of compound interest. I'd like to introduce you to what investment types call the **Rule of 72**. Basically, it states that if your investments are earning a return of 10 per cent, you will double your money every 7.2 years. This is how it the formula works:

Time it will take for your money to double =
72/rate of return

So, if you keep your money in a growth-oriented portfolio (more on that in chapter 7) that is averaging a 12 per cent rate of return, it will take six years for your money to double ($^{72}/_{12} = 6$). On the other hand, if your ordinary savings account is earning 2 per cent, you're looking at thirty-six years to double your money! See what a difference interest can make?

---

* Technically, you could stop making your monthly contribution at 45. However, I would recommend continuing to save. It will increase your financial freedom and flexibility.

Making It Personal

I'm hoping that, by now, you've developed a greater appreciation of what money can do for you—how you can make it work to your advantage, how it can change your life for the better. I'm also hoping that you're sufficiently motivated to dive in and get started. It's never too early (or too late) to take control of your financial future.

Goals Lead and Dreams Follow

Do you have dreams and goals? Of course you do. Have you ever wanted something so badly that you simply had to find a way to get it? Throughout my university years, I dreamed about having my own place when I graduated. For four years I saved a little money each month so that I'd have enough for a small down payment on a townhouse upon graduation. My *goal* of owning a place led me to take *actions* that would make it happen. Now my *dream* of owning a home has come true.

Goals ⟶ Actions ⟶ Dreams

Goals don't have to be huge to be real. Your goal could be to buy a bike next year. Or you may want to complete your post-secondary education with no student debt. To set goals, you must look into your future and figure out where you want to go and what you want to do and have.

What are some of your financial goals?

- _____
- _____
- _____
- _____

This goal business can be tricky. Some goals, like saving for a computer or a car, make perfect sense. Others, like winning the lottery and retiring to Hawaii, may not be so practical. When you set your goals, there are a few things you can do to make sure they have a real chance of happening.

- **Think short and long term:** Sometimes it can take years to have a clear idea of where you want to go, especially when it comes to your money. What do you see for yourself in the future? In particular, how much money do you want to have saved up in one year? In three years? In ten years? In fifty years?

  What do you want to be doing in those same time periods? Jot down your thoughts in the chart below. Committing your goals to paper is like developing a contract with yourself—one that only you can accomplish or break. People who write down their goals are more likely to achieve them than people who do not.

TIME FRAME	PERSONAL GOALS	FINANCIAL GOALS
One year		
Three years		
Ten years		
Fifty years		

- **Create SMART goals:** SMART goals are Specific, Measurable, Attainable, Realistic, and Timely. Rather than writing down a goal that states, "I want to be a millionaire," you might try this: "I want to have $1 million by the time I'm sixty-five using the financial fundamentals and investing techniques I have learned in *Rich by Thirty*." That goal is much clearer than the first and it has all of the elements of a SMART goal. Look at the goals you wrote down on page 26 and in the chart above. Do any of them need to be revised? If so, do that here:

- _____
- _____
- _____
- _____

- **Create a personal vision statement:** Writing a personal vision statement is a huge step toward personal financial success. A vision statement includes both what you want to do in your life and how you are going to do it. A good vision statement will include the following:

  - Who (you!)
  - What (the goal)
  - When (the time frame)
  - How (the action plan)

One of the goals mentioned above was "I want to have $1 million by the time I'm sixty-five using financial fundamentals and investing techniques I have learned in *Rich by Thirty*." Here is an example of a personal vision statement to support that goal:

I, Jane Smith, want to accomplish financial success (over $1 million) by retirement using financial fundamentals that include spending wisely, saving and investing, and giving back to the community.

Writing your personal vision statement can be challenging. Sometimes it's difficult to know where we really want to go in the long term. Most of us, though, at least have some sort of idea. Give it a whirl, and don't worry if it takes a couple of tries to get it right.

_____

_____

_____

_____

If you've got a computer at home, type your vision statement into a program and design a certificate around it. Print it off and frame it. Hang it on your wall so that whenever you see it, you are reminded of the positive direction in which you are headed.

I use my personal vision statement as a reminder of what I want to do with my life. But, as time passes and I change, so do my goals and visions. Don't feel too boxed in by one statement or one set of goals. Make changes to your vision as it becomes clearer through time.

EXCUSES, EXCUSES!

What's holding you back? Make a list of all the reasons you don't think you can get your finances in order. Then, put it somewhere safe and prepare to tear it up in the not-too-distant future. Once you get through the next several chapters, you won't need it anymore, because you'll be on your way. Nothing will hold you back!

Hopefully, you're feeling a little more inspired and motivated than you were when you started reading a few pages back. You know how important it is to start working on your financial future as early as possible, and you know how integral money can be to your future—both short and long term. Now you're ready to put the wheels in motion. You're ready to go out and make it happen!

2
Get Organized:
FILE FOLDERS, BANKS, AND YOU

Organization truly is the key to success. In fact, on the road to wealth and splendour, getting organized is the most important step you'll need to take. Oftentimes this process is referred to as "getting your financial house in order." It may sound a little intimidating, but it's not. It can actually be fun.

The Tools of the Trade

Meet Erica, age twenty-six. She works full-time and rents a small apartment with a roommate. Unfortunately for both of them, Erica has never been very good at managing her money. She never knows how much money she has in her chequing or savings accounts, and her cellphone bills and credit card bills are always stuffed inside her purse or in the glove compartment of her car. Often her bank card and credit cards are declined at stores. Erica jokes with her friends that she doesn't know when her bills are due until her phone service is cut off.

This is funny enough until she gets stuck on the highway with a broken-down car and no cellphone service to enable her to call for help!

Erica needs to get organized! If you read that last paragraph with a sinking feeling in the pit of your stomach, don't worry. It's never too late to start!

File Folders Are Your Friends!

The very first step in your organization process should be a trip to the local office supply store. Head straight to the "file folder" aisle and start shopping. You'll need some multi-coloured file folders and something to keep them in (an accordion case, or one of those desktop hanging folder contraptions will do the trick).

Files are important because they allow you to separate and manage all of the paperwork that pertains to the different areas of your financial and personal life. Filing also gives you an opportunity to review your financial and personal information more carefully.

Here are some examples of file names that might be relevant for you:

- bank statements (if you have more than one account, make a file for each, and include the account number or type on the tab for easy reference)
- utility bills (again, one folder for each utility)
- cellphone bills
- receipts
- credit card bills and related materials
- pay statements/employment information
- tax/government-related materials

- investment statements
- investment information
- health information
- certificates of achievement
- school information

This should be enough to get you started. As you start going through the stacks of important papers in your dresser drawers or on your desk, you'll probably find other materials that should also be given a file. Don't get carried away! You don't need to file every piece of paper that makes its way into your home. A rule of thumb: only file things that are important to you and that could significantly affect your life.

When you organize your brand new files, put them into an order that makes sense to you—alphabetical, most-frequently used, whatever. Just chose a system that will allow you to easily remember where things go.

The Dreaded Spreadsheet

Although some people run screaming at the thought, a truly great way to get organized with your finances is to set up budgets using a computerized spreadsheet program (there will be lots more information on budgets in chapter 3). Most computer operating systems come with a basic spreadsheet program, and that's all you'll really need. It allows you to insert formulas that will add and subtract numbers automatically, or dates that will assist you in planning for certain purchases. I use Excel to keep track of all my income and expenses.

You can also use your computer to create a list of "big-ticket items" that you can work toward purchasing as time progresses. For example, you could include items like a bicycle ($350), car repairs ($900), or a down payment on a new home ($5,000). Put your list someplace where you'll see it on a daily basis (I have mine taped to my desk at home). It will help to motivate you and keep you focused on your goals.

Let Technology Work for You

Getting organized with your investments has become increasingly easier in recent years, thanks to huge advances in Internet technology. Now, all you have to do is log on for a few minutes to check your investments, your bank balances, pay your bills, whatever! Make sure you register for your bank's online services (you'll need to see a customer service representative to do this). If you have started to invest, you can also use the Internet to track the performance of almost any stock, bond, or mutual fund. Two good websites are finance.yahoo.com and www.globeinvestor.com.

These websites, and others like them, include graphs that show the historical performance of your investment. They also include information that will help you determine if a particular investment would be good for you. Some websites even allow you to download data that can be used to create graphs in spreadsheet programs.

Ten Minutes a Week

Getting a handle on your money doesn't take much more than a little planning and checking up once a week. If you're willing to take ten minutes out of your busy week to devote to your financial future, I can guarantee you success. How many hours a day do you spend watching television? If you are like most North Americans in our age group, you are glued to the tube for nearly 3.5 hours a day! That adds up to a stunning 24.5 hours per week!

What's your least favourite show? Can you turn it on ten minutes late, or, better yet, not watch it at all? If you can commit to that, you can spend the time doing something that will really benefit you in the long run. With the ten minutes that you manage to free up, you could:

- Review your banking transactions. This will help you keep track of your expenses and income to ensure that you aren't overspending.
- Brush up your investment skills. Read a book about money management, visit financial websites, read the newspaper!
- Keep tabs on how your investments are doing.
- Set up your automatic banking transactions for the coming week.

The Big Bad Bank

Nineteen-year-old Kumar is in his second year of university. He hides half of his savings underneath the hard drive of his computer. The other half can be found in a small box in his closet. At any given time, he has a stash of more than $9,000 hiding in his room! Because he can easily access his own money, he considers this technique more financially convenient than a bank.

Despite often getting a bad rap, banks are not evil. In fact, a good relationship with a bank that you're comfortable with is a key component in your getting-organized campaign—as important as those multicoloured file folders I recommended above!

As convenient as it may seem to have money sitting under your hard drive, it isn't very safe. There are way too many risks associated with keeping your money "under your mattress" rather than in a bank account. What if your house was robbed? What if your roof leaked? You could lose everything! Besides, if your money is sitting in your closet, it isn't earning interest, is it? And if you read chapter 1 carefully, you now know how important interest can be. The best place for your money is in an account where you can monitor its activity.

Setting up an Account

If you haven't already set up a bank account for yourself, now is the time. The first step is to pick a bank or institution that you would like to deal with. In Canada, the main banks you can deal with are:

- RBC Royal Bank (www.rbcroyalbank.com)
- TD Canada Trust (www.tdcanadatrust.com)
- Scotia Bank (www.scotiabank.com)
- BMO Bank of Montreal (www.bmo.com)
- CIBC (www.cibc.com)

You have other options as well. There are local banks like VanCity Bank in Vancouver or ATB Financial (Alberta Treasury Branch). There are credit unions like the Caisse Populaire in Quebec or Interior Savings in British Columbia. And, in recent years, Internet banks like ING Direct and President's Choice Financial have become increasingly popular.

When selecting a bank, consider location, convenience, policy, and customer service. Check out their websites using the Internet and pay attention to word-of-mouth reputation.

Once you've selected the institution with which you'd like to deal, it's time to set up your accounts. If you are under eighteen, you may need to bring a parent or guardian along. You'll also need at least two pieces of up-to-date identification (a driver's license, birth certificate, passport, or social insurance card, for example). Finally, be aware that some financial institutions require a minimum deposit of up to $50 on the day that you open your account. Once you have all of that in order, an account representative or personal banker will help you to determine what type of account will best suit your needs.

CHEQUING ACCOUNTS A chequing account is designed for activity. Typically, people have their paycheques deposited into it and pay their bills and spend out of it. As the name suggests, you are also able to write cheques on it. A chequing account generally doesn't receive any deposit interest, which makes it less than ideal for long-term savings. Use a chequing account if you are likely to spend your money within two months.

Because of the activity associated with chequing accounts, there is usually a fee to be paid. While I was a student, I had to pay $3.50 each month to use my account. That banking package gave me twenty-five transactions per month and free online banking. Now that I am working full time, I pay $12 per month for my chequing account. For that, I get sixty-five transactions per month, free online banking, and new cheques when I need them.

This usually meets my needs. It's worthwhile looking into these packages when opening an account. Otherwise, you might find yourself paying some hefty fees (up to $1 per transaction)! You can find information about banking packages online or by calling your bank's toll-free customer service number.

SAVINGS ACCOUNTS A savings account is designed to be a place where you can park your money for a longer period of time. You receive interest on the money that you have sitting in this account, but it isn't very much. Generally, it's worth thinking of your savings account as a place to put money that you will have for between two months and one year. For example, I save money for my holidays every year in a savings account, but I don't put my retirement savings there. Savings accounts only have fees associated with them if you use them actively to withdraw money. This is to hinder you from spending your savings. The fees are higher than in the chequing account (up to $1.50 per transaction) making it worth your while not to pull money out too frequently.

I highly recommend that you open both a chequing and a savings account. It's almost impossible to save for the long term in the same account that you use for daily banking activity. Separating your money will make your financial life much easier (you won't accidentally spend your savings!) and help you to develop healthy financial habits.

BANK CARDS AND ONLINE/TELEPHONE ACCESS When you are in the process of opening your chequing and savings accounts, think about whether you want or need a debit card/bank card. This card allows you to pay for your purchases directly at the stores where you shop and gives you bank machine access to your various accounts. It also makes online and telephone banking possible. Bank cards can be wonderfully convenient. Unfortunately, they can also tempt you to spend too much money.

If you're given a choice, I'd recommend getting a card that allows access to your chequing account but not your savings account. This way, you'll have the convenience of accessing your money when you need it, but you won't end up touching your savings. As your comfort level with money increases, you might want to consider allowing yourself access to your savings, but only for the purpose of direct deposits and emergencies.

Lastly, ensure that you have access to online- and telephone-banking services. They are invaluable tools when it comes to automating your investment services.

A BANKING CHECKLIST Here's a quick "to do" list to keep in mind when opening your accounts:

- Choose a bank or institution that suits your needs.
- Make an appointment with a personal banker ahead of time.
- Bring along your mom, dad, or a legal guardian (if under eighteen).
- Bring at least two pieces of current identification.
- Ask to open both a chequing and a savings account.
- Research your bank's service packages and find the one that works for you.
- Be prepared to make a minimum deposit.

- Get a bank card and set it up with access to your chequing account *only*.
- Set up online and telephone banking.

> ### BUYER BEWARE!
> When you visit the bank to open your new accounts, don't be surprised if the personal banker tries to sell you a credit card. Avoid the temptation to sign up—at least for now. You'll find a lot more information on credit in chapter 4.

Fees, Fees, and More Fees

Many people go ballistic over the service fees they pay to their banks. Maybe that's because we all know how much money banks are raking in. Let's face it—at least some of that profit is coming out of your account, if not via fees than through the interest they earn by using your money for their own investments.

It's worth keeping in mind, though, that the fees you pay don't buy a physical product. They buy a service. After all, financial institutions have to staff their various departments in order to serve you and their other clients. They transfer a portion of that cost down to you. Banks that provide a high level of customer service tend to charge higher fees; those that operate on more of a self-serve basis charge less.

To get a clear picture of how this works, let's compare President's Choice Banking (PC) to Royal Bank (RBC). When you bank with PC, an online banking institution, there are no tellers to help you with your transactions.

There are also very few people to answer the phone when you call. There are no physical branches, either. When all is said and done, there is really no "service" at all. Therefore, there are no service fees. On the other hand, RBC offers teller services as well as many other account services. You could, for example, meet with someone to talk specifically about your banking card limits, loans, mortgages, or investments. You can talk to a representative if and when you want. Not surprisingly, this service costs money.

A similar situation exists with brokerage or trading accounts. Let's say you are a very confident investor and you've been investing in the stock market for many years. You make your own investment decisions without the influence of your broker or financial planner. You don't need or want to pay for their advice. You'd be best served by an online trading account that allows you to trade what, when and where you want, all for the relatively low cost of $30 per transaction. An investor with less knowledge and confidence, however, might prefer to use a full-service broker, regardless of the fee (which can be nearly $300 per transaction).

In the end, how you feel about service fees will likely depend on your priorities. Do you value high customer-service levels or not? If you do chose to go with a bank that charges service fees, make sure that you are getting good service for your money. If at any time you feel that you are being let down by the customer service representatives, feel free to speak up. The consumer—regardless of his or her age—is very powerful! Good institutions will recognize and respect that. People in the banking services industry should want to help guide young customers down the path of financial security. If they aren't willing to support you in your banking and investing endeavours, they don't deserve your business.

Advisers and Other Bankers

When you arrive at whichever financial institution you've chosen, a personal banker will assist you in setting up your accounts. Personal bankers can handle most non-transaction account services. For example, they can assist in choosing and setting up the best accounts for your needs, selecting the proper service fee package, and setting up your bank cards. Often, personal bankers will also be able to set up basic investments. They can ask you questions about your long-term and short-term goals that will help determine what basic investments will suit your needs.

By the time you're finished this book, you'll likely be able to start putting together your own financial plan without the help of an adviser. However, when you've got a good handle on the basics, it's great to get some advice from a **financial adviser**. They often share good ideas for your money, and the more information you have, the better. They also tend to approach your personal money management in a very organized manner. Knowledge is a very powerful tool. I highly recommend sitting down with one and working out a financial plan that works for you.

GET A JOB!

So, we've been talking about getting organized and about banking. But what if you don't have any money coming in? The only real way to make money is to work for it. If you don't have an income stream, it is definitely time to get one. Traditionally, we think about working a "regular" job as a means to make money. However, you can think about making money in a variety of ways. Here are a few things you can do:

- Start your own small business
- Trade things on eBay for a profit
- Babysit
- Tutor
- Freelance your services
- Get a job in your field of interest
- Get creative with your investments

If you choose the more traditional path of job hunting, I have a few recommendations: try to work in a field that interests you—you don't want to get yourself into a job that you hate doing; spice up your resumé and cover letters, and customize them to suit the job for which you are looking; read up on proper interviewing and networking techniques. Finally, use all the job hunting resources out there. Online job search engines like Workopolis and Monster will assist you in developing your resumé and cover letter. They also feature many job postings. Some even provide information that will help you determine what career opportunities would be a good match for your skill set and personality.

3
Get Started:

THE JOYS OF BUDGETING

Now that you're organized (or at least on your way to being organized), it's time to start properly managing your money. And the first step in this process is a budget. Unfortunately, budgets have a bad reputation—they're boring, they take a lot of time, they're restricting, etc.

Yup, I'd be in denial if I didn't admit that a lot of people—especially people our age—don't like to think about budgets. Yes, I understand that the whole idea is kind of boring, and it does seem to suggest that huge compromises will need to be made regarding your spending. Well, that second part may be partially true (small compromises will likely need to be made), but budgeting isn't boring; it's essential. A good budget is a vital first step on the road to financial success. Without one, it's next to impossible to know where your money is coming from, or where it's going to. But preparing a budget isn't difficult, and you can think of the exercise as very little pain now for a whole lot of gain later.

DON'T BE LATE!

The only time developing a budget can get tricky is if you do it too late. Let's say you're on a road trip with your friends. You drive for five hours and arrive at the hotel. You pay for the room, go out for a fancy dinner, do some shopping, and put a little more gas in the car. As you merrily spend away, no one stops to think about how much money is left in the "bank." What happens the next day when the car breaks down and you realize you've only got a little cash left? You can avoid this situation by creating a simple budget and sticking to it before you start any adventure.

The 411 on Budgeting

A budget is a financial statement or document that outlines your income and expenditures over a specific period of time. Think of it as a plan for your money—and remember that it doesn't have to be complicated. All you really need to prepare a budget is the spreadsheet program that comes with your computer or some graph paper. To prove just how easy it really is, we're going to walk through the creation of your own personal budget together.

Income and Expenses

First things first. Any budget—be it corporate, household, or personal—begins with an examination of income. Where's the money coming from? For corporations, answering this question can be an extremely complex exercise; for you, it shouldn't be that hard.

Below are a few examples of the "income" portion of a budget. First is the monthly budget of Noor, a seventeen-year-old high school student; second is the monthly budget of Peter, a twenty-five-year-old career person.

Noor (Student)

SOURCES OF INCOME	DOLLARS
Part Time Job	500
Small Side Jobs	50
Total Income	$550

Peter (Young Career Person)

SOURCES OF INCOME	DOLLARS
Full Time Job	2800
Small Side Jobs	50
Total Income	$2,850

So far, so good. Now, think about your situation. Do you have a full- or part-time job? Do you earn an allowance for doing chores around the house? Do you receive a regular GST-rebate cheque from the government? You need to take into account any money that you've got coming in. Now, fill in and total up the "income" portion of your own budget in the worksheet below or in your spreadsheet program.

SOURCES OF INCOME	DOLLARS
Total Income	

Once you have your total income figured out, it's time to look at your expenses. What do you spend money on every month? Be really careful here. You need to think about everything—from big-picture stuff like car loans and rent, to little things like coffee and lunches in the school cafeteria. Keeping track of your expenses is the cornerstone of your financial well-being. One of the top reasons that people (and businesses) go bankrupt is improper cash-flow management. Simply put, more money ends up going out than coming in. Not a good scene!

Let's get back to Noor and Peter and have a look at the "expenditure" portion of their budgets.

Noor (Student)

SOURCES OF EXPENSES	DOLLARS
Clothing	50
Food	50
Savings	50
Entertainment	100
School Expenses	150
Total Expenses	**$400**

Peter (Young Career Person)

SOURCES OF EXPENSES	DOLLARS
Mortgage or Rent	850
Loan	300
VISA	125
Groceries	150
Investment Account	75
Heat	90
Property Tax	120
Electricity	55

Condo Fees	200
Home and Auto Insurance	125
Transit Tickets	70
Vehicle Fuel	120
Subtotal of Mandatory Expenses	**$2,280**
Bank Overdraft	400
Furniture Payment	100
Cellphone Bill	65
Cable, Phone, Internet	125
Gym	32
Subtotal of Secondary Expenses	**$722**
Fun Money	200
Subtotal of Fun Expenses	**$200**
Total Expenses	**$3,202**

A couple of notes on the categories in Peter's budget. **Mandatory expenses** are things that you literally cannot live without. You'll notice that Peter's investments are in this category. Yes, your financial security is indeed this important. **Secondary expenses**, on the other hand, are things that you could live without if push came to shove. They tend to be things that we value, or things that make our lives a bit easier. The **fun expenses** category includes things that are pure luxury; things that make our lives more exciting.

Now it's your turn. Use the worksheet below to fill in your own monthly expenses.

SOURCES OF EXPENSES	DOLLARS
Total Expenses	

We're down to the final piece of the puzzle now—blending the income portion of your budget with the expense portion. Subtract the total expenses from the total income and you're done. Here are our examples, continued:

Noor (Student)

Total Monthly Income	$550
Total Monthly Expenses	$400
Net Income or Loss	$150

Peter (Young Career Person)

Total Monthly Income	$2,850
Total Monthly Expenses	$3,202
Net Income or Loss	$(352)

Noor is doing very well. She's experiencing a net income of $150 every month. If she wants to save for something, or invest for the future, she knows exactly how much money she can use. Peter, on the other hand, isn't faring so well. He's looking at a net monthly loss of $352. Clearly, something's not working. After paying his mandatory expenses each month, there's hardly any money left over. This phenomenon is often called **home poverty**, and it's pretty common for young home owners or renters. To avoid this situation, lifestyle changes are likely needed—a roommate, perhaps, or a move to cheaper accommodations? There will be more information on how to handle this on page 56.

Now it's time to calculate your net income or loss. Fill in the worksheet below, and grab a calculator.

Total Monthly Income
Total Monthly Expenses
Net Income or Loss

How did you do? Are you in a positive position or a negative one? Don't feel bad if your "bottom line" (now you know where that term comes from!) isn't looking great. You're certainly not alone, and part of the reason you bought this book was to help you get control of your financial life, right?

The bottom line of your budget should act as a guide for the next steps in your financial makeover. If the number is negative, you're overspending. In financial circles, this is referred to as a **deficit**, and to say that it's generally frowned upon is an understatement. If, on the other hand, your bottom line is positive, you're in a **surplus** situation— all in all a much happier place to be!

Surpluses are usually produced when a budget allots more money for a specific product or service than is needed in the end. Imagine shopping for a cool, new red hoodie. You've done your research and you know that the hoodie costs $40. You walk into your favourite store and discover that the hoodie is 25 per cent off! Instead of spending $40, you pay $30. You walk out of the store with the hoodie and a $10 surplus in your pocket. Sweet!

The opposite situation occurs when you walk into the same store to find out that the hoodie you saw last week now costs $50. You decide to buy it anyways, and dip into some savings to do so. Now, you've created a $10 deficit.

The income tax process provides another useful example of these concepts. If your employer has taken too much tax off your paycheques throughout the year, you'll probably end up getting a nice return in the mail (a surplus). If he or she hasn't taken enough, you'll end up owing money to the Canada Revenue Agency (a deficit).

So how do you cope with these situations? Read on.

ASSETS AND LIABILITIES

Leave some room at the bottom of your budget spreadsheet to list your assets and liabilities. In financial terms, an **asset** refers to things that you own (like a home, car, money, jewelry, bicycle, or even sports equipment). A **liability** generally refers to something that you owe (tuition, a car loan, a mortgage, a debt). When you subtract your liabilities from your assets, you are left with your **personal net worth**—and there's nothing more exciting like watching it grow over time!

Under-Spending: A Surplus Is a Wonderful Thing

Let's start with the best-case scenario: your budget shows that you've got money left over at the end of each month. Congratulations! What are you going to do? Rush out and treat your ten closest friends to a night on the town? You might be able to afford it, but it wouldn't be the best plan in the long run.

Before visions of extra lattes and thousands of downloads start dancing through your head, think back to chapter 1 and your list of goals. What did you write down on page 26? You are now in the enviable position of having some extra cash to help make those dreams a reality. When we get to chapter 5, we'll talk specifically about how to save for items you want to buy in the short term. For now, simply remember that you should always put aside money when you can afford to do so. Here are a few tips to help get you started.

IT'S OKAY TO REWARD YOURSELF

We've talked a lot about reining in your spending so that you don't cause yourself financial grief. But it's also important to take pride in your income earning ability and reward yourself. Sometimes those rewards come through spending your money on things that are important to you. For example, every year I try to reward myself with a vacation. I find great pleasure in taking a few weeks off and exploring, relaxing, and having fun.

Tips for Dealing with a Surplus

If you are in the fortunate position of having a surplus, here are a few suggestions about what you might do with the extra cash:

- Open a savings account and start saving.
- Start an automated savings plan so that you are saving and/or investing on a regular basis.
- Pay down high-interest debts (see chapter 4).
- Start a college fund.
- Contribute to a down payment for your first home.
- Contribute to a retirement savings account (see chapter 8).
- Reward yourself with part of the surplus...*not* all of it.

Overspending: The Dangers of Deficits

So, you're over your monthly budget. You are spending more than you earn, which might explain why you're always having to borrow bus fare from your parents! What should you do? What can you do? You've got three options: reduce your spending, increase your income, or borrow money. Obviously, this last option isn't always a good one. Let's look at some tips that address the other two.

Tips for Dealing with a Deficit

- **Question everything.** Look carefully at your budget. What are your biggest expenses? Are you spending more money on clothes each month than you need to? Is your car insurance through the roof? Ask yourself if there are lifestyle changes that you can make to reduce your monthly output of cash. Eliminating two pizza dinners each month, for example, could free up $35!

- **Look for opportunities.** Do you have the ability to increase your income? Can you take on a few more hours at work, or make a deal with your parents to do an additional household chore in exchange for an increase in your allowance? Are you driving friends to school every day? Might they be able to contribute a small amount to your gas costs? Do you have a hidden talent that could help you earn some money on the side? These things may seem insignificant, but every little bit helps.

- **Reorganize your priorities.** Put your savings and investing goals at the very top of your list of expenses. These should be non-negotiable—more important to you than a few extra cable channels or an extra night out. Always pay yourself first—even if it's only $25 a month.

- **Examine your cash flow.** As much as we'd like them to be fixed in stone, our expenses change from month to month. This affects your cash flow—a term used to describe the changes that occur in your expenses and income from month to month. You need to be aware of these fluctuations to have a firm grasp on your spending habits. For example, people tend to spend more in December because of the holidays. If you don't budget for this, you might end up with a big credit card bill near the end of January. The opposite situation can occur, as well. Are you taking a two-week holiday from work in the summer? Remember to take your transportation costs off of your budget for that month. The more aware you are of these fluctuations, the better able you'll be to handle them well.

- **Plan for emergencies.** While you're revamping your budget, it's not a bad idea to include an expense dedicated to building an emergency fund. If your car broke down tomorrow, would you have enough money to fix it? If you lost your job next week, how would you cover your expenses until you could find a new one? No one likes to spend more than they have, but things happen. Often, people don't plan for the unexpected. When an emergency occurs, they end up having to work overtime, pay high interest rates on a credit card or do without something that they really need. Some experts recommend that you sock away the equivalent of six month's salary in your own emergency fund. That's a little excessive for the average person, so choose a number that you find comfortable. Then, work it into your short-term savings plan (see chapter 5).

- **Avoid debt.** Only as an absolute last resort should you borrow money to cover your expenses. We'll talk lots more about debt in chapter 4, but for now, just know that borrowing to pay for something you can't really afford is the first step down a very slippery slope. Before long, you'll be borrowing to pay off what you've already borrowed, and so on and so forth. It's much better to look at what you're buying and ask yourself if you really need it. You'll be surprised at how often the answer is no.

Avoiding Home Poverty

When I graduated from university, I bought a townhouse.
I was so excited about having a new job, a new home, living on my own—the whole package! Before too long,
however, I ran right into an extremely common trap: home
poverty. Basically, all I could afford was my house! I didn't
have much money left over for anything else.

On paper, someone like me can make a healthy salary,
but if I don't carefully monitor my cash flow, I could end
up like many North Americans—bankrupt! Let's look at
how this can happen, using Peter from our budget examples as a case study. Peter is twenty-five and works in the
finance department of a local construction company. He
recently bought a small condominium and still has some
student loans to pay off. Although he's got a great job, he's
still running out of money at the end of every month.

Let's look at his budget again to see how and why this
is happening.

Peter in November

SOURCES OF INCOME	DOLLARS
Full-Time Job	$2,800
Small Side Jobs	$50
Total Monthly Income	**$2,850**
SOURCES OF EXPENSES	DOLLARS
Mortgage or Rent	850
Loan	300
VISA	125
Groceries	150
Investment Account	75
Heat	90
Property Tax	120

Electricity	55
Condo Fees	200
Home and Auto Insurance	125
Transit Tickets	70
Vehicle Fuel	120
Subtotal of Mandatory Expenses	**$2,280**
Bank Overdraft	0
Furniture Payment	100
Cellphone Bill	65
Cable, Phone, Internet	125
Gym	32
Subtotal of Secondary Expenses	**$322**
Fun Money	200
Subtotal of Fun Expenses	**$200**
Total Expenses	**$2,802**
Total Monthly Income	$2,850
Total Monthly Expenses	$2,802
Net Income or Loss	**$48**

As you can see, Peter is managing to juggle all of his payments, and he even has a little extra money for himself. In November, at least, he doesn't have an overdraft in his bank account. In December, however, things take a turn for the worse.

Peter in December

SOURCES OF INCOME	DOLLARS
Full-Time Job	$2,800
Small Side Jobs	$50
Total Monthly Income	**$2,850**
SOURCES OF EXPENSES	DOLLARS
Mortgage or Rent	850

Loan	300
VISA	125
Groceries	150
Investment Account	75
Heat	90
Property Tax	120
Electricity	55
Condo Fees	200
Home and Auto Insurance	125
Transit Tickets	70
Vehicle Fuel	120
Subtotal of Mandatory Expenses	**$2,280**
Bank Overdraft	0
Furniture Payment	100
Cellphone Bill	65
Cable, Phone, Internet	125
Gym	32
Subtotal of Secondary Expenses	**$322**
Holiday Gifts	500
Fun Money	200
Subtotal of Fun Expenses	**$700**
Total Expenses	**$3,302**
Total Monthly Income	$2,850
Total Monthly Expenses	$3,302
Net Income or Loss	**$(452)**

Ah, the holidays! You'll notice that Peter has spent a whopping $500 on holiday gifts in the month of December—a "fun expense" that has turned his bottom line from a positive to a negative. It's too bad that Peter didn't think ahead, and plan for this expense (after all, it's not like he didn't know the holidays were coming), because this seemingly small outlay of cash has a bit of a snowball effect. Check out what happens in January.

Peter in January

SOURCES OF INCOME	DOLLARS
Full-Time Job	2,800
Small Side Jobs	50
Total Monthly Income	**$2,850**

SOURCES OF EXPENSES	DOLLARS
Mortgage or Rent	850
Loan	300
VISA	125
Groceries	150
Investment Account	75
Heat	90
Property Tax	120
Electricity	55
Condo Fees	200
Home and Auto Insurance	125
Transit Tickets	70
Vehicle Fuel	120
Subtotal of Mandatory Expenses	**$2,280**
Bank Overdraft	452
Furniture Payment	100
Cellphone Bill	65
Cable, Phone, Internet	125
Gym	32
Subtotal of Secondary Expenses	**$774**
New Year Sale Purchases	300
Fun Money	200

Subtotal of Fun Expenses	$500
Total Expenses	$3,554
Total Monthly Income	$2,850
Total Monthly Expenses	$3,554
Net Income or Loss	$(704)

Not surprisingly, Peter's net loss has increased. Why? Because he hasn't made any lifestyle changes that would allow him to reduce his debt. Instead of curbing his shopping in January, for example, he goes out and takes advantage of the sales. Instead of using his fun money to pay down his debt from December, he spends it the same way he always does. If Peter continues to spend at this rate, his debt will continue to grow. And the worst part of all is that even if he did stop his "extra" spending, his normal budget doesn't really allow him to start paying off the debt. It's quite likely that Peter will end up carrying this debt for a long while—racking up interest charges along the way.

Scary, isn't it? Peter offers a perfect example of what can happen if you don't set realistic budgets and stick to your cash-flow goals. As you can see, the amount of money "lost" increases every month. And he isn't making any real progress with paying down the money that he owes at the bank, either. He can't pay off his existing debt before a new pile plows him over each month. Debt builds on top of debt, thus creating more debt. If Peter continues in this vein, spending the same amount of money each month and not making any lifestyle changes, a bleak picture begins to emerge. He will borrow more and more money, dip into his savings, sell any assets he might have, and end up deeper and deeper in debt.

Surprisingly, many people find these "solutions" easier than making some obviously needed lifestyle changes. But changing the way that you live is by far the most effective solution! Here are some ideas to help get you started, and there will be more information on living frugally in chapter 5:

- **Consider finding a roommate** with whom you can split the rent/mortgage, utilities, and grocery bills.
- **Follow recommended heating and electricity practices** to help reduce your monthly bills. For example, turn off your lights and computer before you head off for work. Also, ensure you have the proper weather stripping on all of your doors and windows.
- **Cut the cable.** As painful as this may seem, cable isn't a necessity. Grab a book or borrow some movies from the library.
- **Perform your own maintenance.** You'd be surprised how many people pay others to do things that they could actually do themselves. Hey, if you feel entrepreneurial you could make money doing other people's housecleaning, lawn maintenance, leaf raking, or snow shovelling.
- **Downsize.** eBay is a wonderful way to get rid of things you don't need—and gain a little extra income in the process.
- **Buy used.** If you need to replace something in your home, consider purchasing it used. Often times you can save hundreds if not thousands of dollars.

We've touched on debt a little bit in this chapter, but it really is a key concept. Before we talk more specifically about how to save and invest your hard-earned cash, let's spend a little more time trying to understand how not to get caught in the credit crunch.

4

Get Out from Under:

AVOIDING THE CREDIT CRUNCH

If there's one thing that can put the brakes on a good financial plan, it's a whopping pile of debt. Let's take a few minutes to examine the debt factor: why we're in it, how to pay it down if we are, and, perhaps most importantly, how to avoid it altogether!

The Money Pit

Money seriously doesn't grow on trees. As obvious as this may seem, our under-thirty generation spends as if it does. Since 1989, disposable income (the income left over after you've paid your taxes) has grown only 1.8 per cent annually. Consumer spending, on the other hand, has grown at an annual rate of 2.6 per cent. Clearly, we're spending way more than we earn—and racking up huge amounts of debt along the way. Scary!

So what does all of this mean in dollar figures? In North America, the youth market spends more than

$112.5 billion each year, and we have a huge influence on household purchases. The average twelve- to thirteen-year-old has $1,500 to spend each year, while the average sixteen- to seventeen-year-old spends $4,500. Over the age of seventeen, figures vary greatly due to educational or career choices. Typically, young people have more spending money than their parents or guardians (who tend to pay for things like housing, heat, and electricity out of their earnings).

Because the youth market has relatively few financial obligations, we tend to spend our money on things that we want, and rarely on things that we need. Consider Anne, a typical sixteen-year-old still living at home. Her parents or guardians buy her clothes and food, and pay for her shelter. She may even be given an allowance for doing things around the house. With virtually none of her needs neglected, Anne has the opportunity to spend her money on whatever it is that she wants. (On the opposite end of the spectrum, of course, a struggling young student may face an entirely different situation. His money may go to things like groceries, rent, tuition, and books. Chances are his budget is very tight.)

But back to the sixteen- or seventeen-year-old for a moment. If we take that $4,500 as an accurate figure, it breaks down to approximately $375 of spending money each month. Where is all this cash going?

How We Get Sucked In

Keaton, seventeen, and Claire, sixteen, have been dating for about six months. On the weekends—when they aren't cramming in their homework—you can usually find them at the mall. They both love to shop for music, clothes, and whatever *else they feel like buying! After a full day of power shopping, they often join their other friends for dinner and a movie. It isn't uncommon for each of them to spend $80 every weekend.*

Like Keaton and Claire, many young people are spending the bulk of their money at the mall! We tend to visit the mall at least once a week and spend an average of $46.80 each time. Add that up over the course of a year, and we're spending $2,433.60!

Why are we spending so much? There are some very powerful marketing and advertising forces out there! The amount of money spent on retail advertising has increased every year for decades. Between 2003 and 2004, for example, advertisers increased their budgets by 17 per cent. No wonder we're compelled to shop! Advertising messages are extremely convincing and they all say the same thing: "You *need* to have this service or product, and you need to have it *now*."

Essentially, our generation ends up trapped in debt because of so-called retail therapy. Swayed by all of this advertising, we shop to make ourselves happy. We watch beer commercials and think that if we drink that brand, we'll live that kind of life. We buy skin cream because we want to look like the model in the ad. We're chasing the dreams that the advertising companies put out there for us, and we like doing it! We tend to be happy with our purchases—at least until that credit card bill arrives in the mail.

Although marketing and advertising forces are strong, you can turn the tables and use them to your advantage— as a source of knowledge rather than persuasion. When you're in the market for a vehicle, for example, do some research into what's out there. Use advertisements to find out more about the vehicle (price, safety, quality, etc.). You can then compare models and brands. With any medium and large product or service that you want to purchase, it is a good idea to do some research and get the facts so that you can make the best decision.

Shopping around can actually be fun. When I was in university, my friend Laura was in the market for a car. She had been driving around in a "beater" for years and finally had saved enough to purchase a quality used car. Laura took a few months to make her decision about what vehicle to buy. She searched the Internet for quality and safety ratings. She spoke with friends that had vehicles she might be interested in. She test drove her "picks" a number of times. Slowly, she narrowed down her search to her two favourite cars. Then she began speaking with dealerships and private owners about price. She chose an Acura RSX and got an absolutely great deal. Because she didn't buy new, she saved money. Because she took the time to negotiate, she saved money. Lastly, because she did her research, she saved money by not getting ripped off. Laura is now a very happy car owner who didn't have to break the bank to get what she wanted.

Debt, Debt, and More Debt: The Dangers of Interest

So we've established that spending money is fun—we like to buy things that we want and need! And it's clear that most of us are pretty good at it, too! All we need to do is think of something we want, find it, purchase it, and voila, the money is spent.

That's the happy side of the coin. The scary side is that we often don't have the money needed to make the purchase in question. But we make the purchase anyway. How? We go into debt.

Because credit is so readily available, we've become very comfortable with the idea of owing money. Most of us have credit cards, and we don't hesitate to use them. We live in a buy-now–pay-later society, and we fully expect to get the things we crave without having to wait or save up. We throw the purchase on the credit card and have to work extra hours so that we can pay for our fancy new items. What's worse, these fancy new items end up costing us more than we should really be paying. If we can't pay the bill in full at the end of the month, the credit card company charges us interest, usually between 18 and 20 per cent! Now, that happy feeling we got from instant gratification has forced us into a situation where we are continually paying for the past rather than investing in the future! Doesn't feel so good anymore, does it?

Let's take a minute to really look at this phenomenon. Let's say that you purchase a few new outfits from your favourite store at a cost of $600. Let's also say that you pay for it with your credit card. The minimum payment on the bills that you receive is likely about $45 (depending on your interest rate—most credit cards average about 19 per cent). If you make only that minimum payment, you'll barely be covering the interest! Almost none of your payment will go toward the principal amount owing. If you were to stick to this approach—paying only the minimum each month—it would take you between fifteen to twenty months to pay off that initial $600. Even worse, the "true" cost of your borrowing (principal plus interest paid) could be anywhere between $675 to $900!

If, however, you can pay off your balance within thirty days, you don't pay any interest at all. Before you whip out that card, think about whether or not you can afford to pay it off. If it's going to take you months to clear your balance, you might want to hold off on your purchase.

WHEN IS A CREDIT CARD A GOOD THING?

Credit cards aren't all bad. They can be very useful in building your **credit rating**. Your credit rating is something you will need when you start thinking about making a big purchase like a house or a car. To borrow money, you have to have proof that you are responsible enough to pay it off. A credit card offers a good opportunity for you to show potential creditors that you can indeed manage debt.

Credit cards also enable us to book vacations, shop online, pay tuition, and so on. And they can be very useful if you ever run into trouble. For example, my car broke down one summer about five hundred kilometres from my home. I used my credit card to pay the mechanic. I made it home safely and paid off my bill with my next paycheque.

Digging Your Way Out

Mike is a twenty-four-year-old electrician's apprentice. When he was between eighteen and nineteen years old, he managed to rack up about $21,200 in debt. He got himself into a lot of financial trouble that has made it very difficult for him to borrow at good interest rates. He is still paying off his debt.

Does Mike's situation sound familiar to you? Have you gotten yourself in over your head? Are you looking at a pile of credit card bills with no idea of how to pay them off? First, I'd suggest that you go back and reread the sections on living the frugal life. Trust me, it will help. The basic idea, though, is this: you need to reduce your expenses to free up some cash. Once you free up the cash, you can start paying down the debt. (Oh, and cut up that card before you get yourself into any more trouble!)

The debt-reduction strategy we're going to work through over the next few pages is designed for individuals who are really squeezed for cash. It's also dead simple. Get ready. A debt-free future is within reach.

STEP 1: FIND A ROLL OF WRAPPING PAPER. Yup, wrapping paper. Get your hands on some old, forgotten roll that's lurking in the back of a closet. Roll out a two to three foot section and tape it to your wall (coloured side in!).

STEP 2: IDENTIFY YOUR DEBTS. Now, take a pen and write down all of your debts—credit cards, loans, the $10 your buddy lent you last week. Then, underneath each item, note the interest rate, the starting balance, and the minimum payment due. Let's use Mike, from above, as a working example. His table is below. Yours will end up looking similar.

	VISA	AMERICAN EXPRESS	CAR LOAN	STUDENT LINE OF CREDIT
Interest Rate (%)	19.50	18.50	9.50	5.90
Starting Balance	$1,200	$1,000	$9,000	$10,000
Minimum Payment	$65	$35	$150	$200

As you put this table together, pay particular attention to the interest-rate row. If you're like most people who find themselves in debt, you are more focused on the amount owing than on the interest rate. This is a common mistake. It may be more gratifying to pay off the smaller debts first, but if you're paying more interest on the larger debts, it is wise to turn your attention to those at the outset (more on this in Step 4, below).

STEP 3: MAKE DEBT REDUCTION PART OF YOUR BUDGET. Now the fun part starts. Every month, you need to make sure that you're in a position to make at least your monthly payments. To do this, you must place these minimum payments at the very top of your monthly budget. In Mike's case, he's looking at a total debt reduction expense of $450 per month ($65 + $35 + $150 + $200). So go ahead and make those payments. Put an X underneath any debt that you made your regular payment on.

STEP 4: MAKE USE OF YOUR SPARE CHANGE. Next, you need to turn your attention to the debt with the highest interest rate. Each month, do your absolute best to put a little extra toward this debt—even as little as $20 will help. In Mike's example, he'd want to put his extra cash toward his VISA bill. The interest rate, at 19.5 per cent, is the highest of the bunch. A great trick to learn about extra payments is to space them so that they are made approximately two weeks after your first payment. Because of the way interest rates are calculated (especially credit cards), you can significantly reduce the amount of time it takes to pay off your debt.

STEP 5: ONE DOWN, THREE TO GO. Once you've paid off the highest-interest-bearing debt, you can pat yourself on the back and move on to the next highest-interest charger! For Mike, it's American Express. He'd go back to Step 3 and do the whole thing all over again, making the minimum payment on everything and throwing any extra money onto his American Express card two weeks after the minimum payment. This time, however, finding that little bit of extra cash shouldn't be as hard—after all, Mike's just freed himself from having to pay VISA every month. In fact, he's got an extra $65 to spend these days. Once he pays off the American Express, he can go back and narrow it down even further.

That's it! It's really that simple. The chart on page 72 is a condensed version of a chart that spans over the course of four years and shows two payments each month. This is just one example of how this method of debt reduction can work. It might take more or less time for you, depending on your unique situation. Your minimum payments may also be different. The great thing about this chart, however, is that you can adapt it to suit your needs.

Ultimately, the best solution to debt reduction is to not get into debt in the first place. Or, avoid accumulating more debt while you are reducing your old debt. If you can avoid debt, you'll end up having more available cash flow. More cash for you means more options. The more options and choices you have, the more freedom you have. Keep in mind that it is super easy to spend $1000. I could do it in a half an hour. But it is much harder to pay it back!

Condensed Payment Plan

	VISA	AMERICAN EXPRESS	CAR LOAN	STUDENT LINE OF CREDIT
Interest Rate (%)	19.50	18.50	9.50	5.90
Starting Balance	$1,200	$1,000	$9,000	$10,000
Minimum Payment	$65	$35	$150	$200
1-Jun-06	X	X	X	X
15-Jun-06	$30	N/A	N/A	N/A
1-Jul-06	X	X	X	X
15-Jul-06	$30	N/A	N/A	N/A
1-Aug-06	X	X	X	X
15-Aug-06	$30	N/A	N/A	N/A
1-Mar-07	GONE	X	X	X
15-Mar-07	GONE	$65	N/A	N/A
1-Apr-07	GONE	X	X	X
15-Apr-07	GONE	$65	N/A	N/A
1-May-07	GONE	X	X	X
15-May-07	GONE	$65	N/A	N/A
1-Dec-07	GONE	GONE	X	X
15-Dec-07	GONE	GONE	$100	N/A
1-Jan-08	GONE	GONE	X	X
15-Jan-08	GONE	GONE	$100	N/A
1-Feb-08	GONE	GONE	X	X
15-Feb-08	GONE	GONE	$100	N/A
1-Feb-09	GONE	GONE	GONE	X
15-Feb-09	GONE	GONE	GONE	$225
1-Mar-09	GONE	GONE	GONE	X
15-Mar-09	GONE	GONE	GONE	$225
1-Apr-09	GONE	GONE	GONE	X
15-Apr-09	GONE	GONE	GONE	$225
1-May-09	GONE	GONE	GONE	GONE

X = Regular Payment

N/A = No Extra Payments

CONSOLIDATION

If your debt situation is really, really bad, you might want to consider a **consolidation loan**. A consolidation loan is where all your debts are wrapped into one loan at a lower interest rate, allowing you to make one monthly payment instead of three or four or more. I highly recommend talking to your personal banker about whether or not you could qualify. They are sometimes difficult to get, but if you don't ask, you'll never know.

The key with a consolidation loan is to not get into any additional debt while you are making payments. You don't want to pay off your loan for three years and have to get another one because you haven't been responsible with your money.

A Little More Information on Biweekly Payments

We talked briefly about this above, but the biweekly payment plan is worth spending a little more time on—especially if you're dealing with a large debt.

Reducing your debt with biweekly payments allows you to put more of your coin on the principal amount owing, rather than on the accrued interest. By doing so, you end up reducing your debt faster than you would if you made one combined principal plus interest payment each month.

Let's say that you're carrying a $40,000 balance on your credit card (extreme, I know, but it will help make a point). On that amount of debt, your minimum monthly payment would be at least $850. With an interest rate of

19.5 per cent, about $750 of that payment would be applied to interest penalties and only $100 to the principal debt. At that rate, you'd be looking at nearly six years' worth of payments before you were debt free!

For argument's sake, let's say that you paid $1,000 a month each month for the first year. By the end of the twelve-month period, your remaining balance would be $35,354.69. A little depressing, considering that you've put $12,000 onto your credit card!

Now let's look at what happens if you pay $500 every two weeks instead. By the end of the twelve-month period—after twenty-six payments—your remaining balance would be $34,287.81. The difference is noticeable: $1,066.88.

If you follow this to its natural conclusion, with bi-weekly payments all the way through, you'll end up paying approximately $6,000 less over four years. And you'll save time as well. With monthly payments, you'll need five years and five months to pay off your debt; with biweekly, you're looking at four years and nine months.

By the way, an accelerated biweekly payment is also very beneficial with other large debts, like mortgages and car payments. An accelerated biweekly payment is similar to a biweekly payment, but the difference is that your payment is slightly higher. The increase in the payment tends to be an insignificant amount of money, sometimes an additional $15 to $50 per payment. The great thing about this insignificant increase is that it has a significant impact on the amount of time it takes you to pay off your debt. For example, if you purchase a home with a twenty-five-year mortgage, an accelerated biweekly payment will reduce your amortization period (the amount of time you'll be paying off the loan!). For instance, if you bought a home for $200,000 with a twenty-five-year mortgage, you'd need to make three hundred equal payments of $1,000 each to pay it off (twelve payments each year). If you switch to an accelerated biweekly payment of one-half the regular monthly amount—$500 every two weeks—you end up making twenty-six payments each year. Instead of paying a yearly total of $12,000 , you're now looking at $13,000 toward your loan. You've literally added one monthly mortgage payment each year! If the interest rate stays with the historical average of 8 per cent over the years, you will end up paying off your mortgage in nineteen or twenty years rather than twenty-five, which is the historical average. Neat trick!

In the example above, it is important to note that accelerated biweekly payments don't always work for everyone. If your money is really tight, as in you've budgeted down to the last $15 or $50, it might not be possible to take advantage of this trick. I'd recommend that as your financial situation improves over time (*Rich by Thirty* will play a key role in this), and you start making more money, switch to an accelerated biweekly payment and take advantage of the opportunity to reduce the amount of time it takes for you to pay off your loan.

So what's the bottom line? The best way to avoid debt is to start living the frugal life and to focus on saving for your future. By making your savings a priority, you'll be motivated enough to overcome the temptations of debt. Remember, you are saving for your financial well-being—for your own goals and dreams. In the next chapter, we're going to get specific about how to do just that.

5

Get Saving:

RIGHT HERE, RIGHT NOW

Saving money is different from investing money. You save money for things you want in the short term—things like a vacation, new computer, bicycle, or a down payment on a home or vehicle. Investing is for the long term. Think retirement.

If you are diligent about saving, you can indeed have the things you want. And because of the short time frame, it's actually a pretty rewarding process. For example, throughout university, I saved money toward a very small down payment on a home. When I graduated, all my scrimping and saving paid off when I got to enjoy my new townhouse. Investing is also rewarding, but it is harder to see your end goal if your time horizon is forty years down the road.

So, let's think about saving as something you do for things you'd like to achieve within one to three years. You might, for example, save for a vacation over the course of two years by depositing money into your savings account every time you get paid. You'll only earn a little bit of interest this way, but there's no risk involved. The money that you put in will be there when you're ready to take it out.

Saving 101

Eighteen-year-old Rebecca is getting ready to head off to university in the fall. She's been attempting to save her money so that she can buy a new laptop for her studies. After a few months of trying, she has given up! She just can't seem to make progress. Now, school is just two months away, and if she's going to get a laptop, she's going to have to borrow some coin to do so.

Does Rebecca's story sound familiar? Do you have any idea what she's doing wrong? If you've read chapter 2, you know that she's not approaching her goals in an organized way. She doesn't have a plan for action, and that's bound to lead to disappointment. To successfully save, you need to have a clear sense of your goals, and a plan for getting there.

Like investing, which we'll discuss in chapters 6 and 7, savings requires some dedication. With so many tempting products on the market these days, it is difficult to save! You could easily blow through $1,000 at the mall in two hours—but it could take a full year to put that money back into your savings account. Yes, it's challenging to *not* give in to temptations, but the end result will be great. Down the road, you will have more money than most people your age. And that money will help you make your dreams realities.

Making It Work: The Frugal Life

Meet Aaliyah. She's a twenty-one-year-old university student who works part time as a server at a restaurant. Luckily, her job pays well. She can cover her tuition fees and still save a little each month. To do this, however, she has to live a pretty frugal life. She packs a lunch and only buys coffee once or twice a week. She borrows books, movies, and magazines from the library rather than buying them. She hits up the second-hand stores for her clothing. All of this is worth it, though. When Aaliyah is finished her degree, she will have saved about $4,000—enough to take a trip or make a down payment so she can start living on her own!

The key to being smart with your money is to live the frugal life. Now don't panic! This doesn't mean you have to penny pinch with absolutely everything. But it does mean that you must be conscious of what you're spending and—more importantly—*why*. If you want to get a handle on your money, get a handle on your spending!

FRUGAL FUNDAMENTALS "Spend your money wisely." How many times have you heard that phrase? Was the person saying it a generation or two older than you? Don't let that fact change your opinion. Despite what you may or may not want to believe, the phrase does have a lot of value. My friend Erin is the queen of frugal living. Over the years she has given some great advice on being frugal (even to me) and some great tips on saving money. Together, we've developed a list of tips and tricks to help you live the frugal life:

- **Be Ruthless.** Before you plunk down your hard-earned cash, ask yourself whether you really need the item in question, or if you just want it. If you don't need yet another pair of strappy sandals, or a new set of speakers for your stereo, then you might want to reconsider its priority on your shopping list. Having trouble sorting it out? Try waiting twenty-four hours before buying. Often, you'll change your mind.

- **Cut the Credit.** If your credit card is getting you into trouble, hide it! Get it out of your wallet. Give it to a parent or trusted adult to hold, or stick it in a re-sealable bag, fill the bag with water, and put the whole package in the freezer. By the time your cards have thawed, you'll have had a chance to think twice about making that "must have" purchase—and don't bother trying to hammer the ice; it will just wreck the cards.

- **Wheel and Deal.** Everything is negotiable. If you feel your credit card interest rate is too high, call and talk about it with a customer service representative. Negotiate better rates on your debt, on your cell-phone bill, on your Internet service. Remember, if you don't ask, you don't get.

- **Pare Down.** While you're in that wheeling and dealing mode, why not take a close look at your various plans. Do you really need all those cable channels, or that many hours of Internet access each month? Do you need text messaging and voice mail on your cell-phone? Think hard, and get rid of anything you don't need.

- **Become a Bargain Hunter.** Look for sales and discounts when you shop. Check out eBay, auctions, garage sales, and estate sales. I've done it and had great success. My dining room table cost $50, my TV

stand was $8, my stove was $60, and my two beauti-
ful leather couches cost a total of $500! My grand
total was $618. Had I purchased these items new, I
would have paid nearly $3,500. You can also check
out vintage stores for cool clothes, jewelry, and
accessories.

- **Entertain Yourself on the Cheap.** Don't forget to
apply the bargain-hunter rules to other areas of your
life. If you enjoy going out for dinner and to the
movies, keep your eyes open for coupons or two-for-
one nights, or get to know the discount theatres in
your neighbourhood. Better yet, why not host a
potluck and video night for your friends? Did you
know that most public libraries have a great collec-
tion of videos and DVDs? Yes, renting is cheaper than
the theatre, but borrowing is free! (Hint: they loan
CDs as well!)

- **Think about Your Food Habits.** We spend a ton of
money on food, whether we live with our parents or
on our own. Here are a few ideas for everyone to
keep in mind:
  - If you live at home, eat at home—or pack a
  lunch! Fast food is a budget killer and can add up
  to over $100,000 throughout your lifetime.
  - Stop drinking pop. You'll have more money and
  you'll be healthier.
  - Try cutting back on meat (vegetarian dishes are
  often cheaper to prepare).
  - Buy your food in bulk (the more you buy, the
  cheaper it gets).
  - And finally, trade in your "designer" coffee for a
  less expensive cup! (Better yet, buy a travel mug

and bring your own hot beverage wherever you are going.)

- **Get Healthy.** A healthy lifestyle can be remarkably affordable. Just think about it: if you drink or smoke, cutting down can put dollars back into your pocket and add years to your life. Walking or biking instead of driving or taking public transit will leave you feeling fit both physically and financially. Why not give it a try for a week and see what kind of difference it makes?

COMMIT YOURSELF!

Many successful financial advisers suggest saving at least 10 per cent of everything you earn.

I think it's possible to save even more. If you are working and living on your own, why not aim for 20 per cent? (I've been sticking to this goal for years now.) If you're living at home and are without expenses such as a mortgage or rent, I challenge you to save 50 per cent. You'll never have another opportunity to save this much again. Think about what you save each month. Commit to something that is realistic and write it in below:

I, _____, commit to saving _____ every month or every paycheque.

It is important to put your savings commitment above all of your other financial commitments. Pay yourself first because no one else will!

Simple, right? Sort of. It's not easy to change your lifestyle or to cut back on things that you really like, but it's worth it in the end. Think about it this way. If you were to cut out one fancy $3 coffee each weekday (you could treat yourself on weekends, if you absolutely had to!), you'd free up approximately $60 a month! That's $60 you could put toward your savings—for those shoes, that vacation, or a new car. It's your choice.

So, now that you've actually figured out how to free up some money, what do you do with it? Keep reading.

Making It Work

Meet Christopher, nineteen. His best friends are planning a ski trip to Whistler in twelve months. Christopher's parents have said that he can go if—and only if—he pays for the trip himself. With just one year to save, Christopher is a little nervous! He doesn't even know where to start.

With money, as with almost anything, the trick is to break things down into the basics. Christopher has one year to save $1,000. If you look at the year in terms of months, this means that Christopher has to tuck away about $83 per month. Because he lives at home with his parents and has very few expenses, saving that amount each month seems pretty reasonable. However, as we've already learned, saving money can be difficult. What if his car dies, or the speakers he really wants go on sale?

One way to ensure that you don't get distracted from your savings goals is to commit yourself to a plan. By following a few easy steps, you'll be able to stick to that plan and achieve your savings goals.

- **Step 1: Write down Your Goals.** As we learned in chapter 1, it's much easier to stick to a plan if it's written down somewhere. In Christopher's case, he'd simply write, "I want to save $1,000 for a ski vacation in one year's time."

- **Step 2: Do the Math.** Once you know what you want and when you want it, you can do some more specific number crunching. For example, if Christopher needs to save $1,000 over one year, he should put away $83 a month for the next twelve months ($1,000/12 months = $83 per month).

- **Step 3: Open a Savings Account.** If you don't already have one, open up a savings account that has a reasonable rate of return (they tend to vary from about 0.05 to 2.5 per cent). When you speak to the bank representative, make sure that the account is set up as "deposit only." This will ensure that you cannot take money out of the account using your debit card. (When you've reached your savings goal, you can remove this designation, and allow yourself to access the money.)

- **Step 4: Automate Your Monthly Savings Contribution.** Have your financial institution automatically take your savings money from your chequing account on the day that you get paid. This automates your deposit so that you don't have to do it yourself. You won't forget, and you won't be tempted to spend your money elsewhere. Most importantly, you'll be paying yourself first. In the box on page 81, I mentioned how important this is. You should be the number one financial priority in your life…not your creditors. If you don't put aside your savings and investing funds first, no one else will.

Christopher did manage to save his $1,000 in twelve months. He followed the steps outlined above and got his savings into gear. Christopher also lived pretty frugally! He saved about $30 a week by not buying lunch every day (he allowed himself a lunch out once a week as a treat). He put that savings towards his ski trip and even had a little bit of money left over. Because he worked so hard to save his money, Christopher thoroughly enjoyed himself. He earned it!

GET AUTOMATED!

Automated banking services are handy for all sorts of reasons. Every time I get paid, my employer deposits money into my bank account. On that same day, my savings and investing money is electronically transferred from my chequing account into the next appropriate account. I also have my bills set up to be paid electronically on the day that they are due. This lets me keep my money in my bank account until I must make a payment. I am gaining interest on that amount while I wait for the due date. These electronic transfers don't take much of my time at all because I set them up ahead of time. The only thing I do is check up on my financial situation for about ten minutes every week.

What Are You Saving For?

When you imagine yourself one to three years down the road, what tangible things do you see? Do you own a particular vehicle or live in a certain community? Perhaps you see yourself pursuing your education. Write down some of your visions for the not-too-distant future. In particular, identify some of the things for which you'd like to save.

_____

_____

_____

_____

_____

Now, go back and pencil in a price beside each item you wrote down. You may have to look on the Internet or grab a newspaper to make sure you're being realistic about this.

Got it? Okay. Let's just say that the first item on your list is a car, and let's say that you're being pretty honest about the whole thing. You know that the newest BMW is not likely going to be sitting in your driveway three years from now, so you're going to focus on something older, maybe even a little rundown. Something you can use to get from point A to point B. Nothing fancy, just practical. Let's say you're budgeting $6,000 for this new used car.

But there's also item number two. Let's say that your family computer is ancient, and you know that you're going to need a new one to keep up with your school work. Unlike the car, which can wait a bit, you'd really like that computer in two years. And you figure it's going to cost you $2,000.

So, you know what you want. Let's do some math and figure out what it's going to take to get it for you. The key thing is to figure out how much you're going to need to save each month. You do this according to a monthly savings formula, which looks like this:

purchase price/number of months until purchase date = monthly savings

For the computer, the formula goes like this:

$2,000/24 months = $83.33 per month

And for the car:

$6,000/36 months = $166.67 per month

To purchase both things, you'd need to save $250 a month ($83.33 + $166.67) for the next twenty-four months. At that point, you could buy your computer and continue saving $166.67 a month for the next twelve months. At the end of that period, you'd have enough for your car as well.

How much will you have to save each month so that you can have some of the bigger things that you want? You can try this calculation with the savings items that you have listed above. Just take the purchase price and divide it by the number of months in which you want to have that item. Your result will tell you how much money you need to save every month to make your goal a reality.

Item 1: _____

_____ (purchase price)/_____ (months) = _____
(savings per month)

Item 2: _____

_____ (purchase price)/_____ (months) = _____
(savings per month)

Item 3: _____

_____ (purchase price)/_____ (months) = _____
(savings per month)

How did you do? Sometimes, we find that the items we want cost more than we thought—or that it will take us much longer to save for them than we imagined. If you found that your monthly savings amount was too high for your budget, try extending the amount of time it takes to save by increasing the number of months that you put into your calculation. On the flip side, perhaps you've found that your monthly savings amount was less than you expected! If that's the case, you might be able to save more every month and so, you can shorten your time horizon by reducing the amount of months that you put into your calculation.

One of the most rewarding experiences you can have is spending your hard-earned savings on your own goals. Enjoy it and enjoy your rewards!

Bumps in the Road

Pedro has been working a part-time job since he was sixteen. He is now twenty and has been saving his money at a rate of $150 per month for the past four years. He now has about $7,200 to put towards a vehicle. However, when an overseas relative passed away, he needed to attend the funeral. He had no choice but to dip into his savings account for a plane ticket, a new suit, accommodations, flowers and meals. Now, he's down about $3,000, and he's pretty much given up on his dreams of owning a vehicle for another two years.

Life brings about some unexpected changes—changes that can affect both your ability and motivation to save. However, when it comes to your financial health, you've got to roll with the punches and carry on. If you don't, you aren't going to achieve your goals. Here are a few things that you can do when the unexpected happens:

- **Recognize when your plans are getting off track.** The only way you'll be able to do this is to be organized with your money. Use tools like online banking to keep track of where money is going and why. You might be able to recognize a nasty trend before it depletes your entire savings.
- **Never give up.** Even when you are discouraged, don't give up on your financial dreams. You will never achieve them if you do.
- **Get back into your healthy financial habits.** If you've been forced to veer from a savings plan, start it up again as soon as you are able. Don't let a temporary twist in the road become permanent.

- **Be proactive, not reactive.** Try to predict as best you can what events will impact your finances and plan for them in advance. For example, if you know you have to pay for tuition in a year, brace yourself for the expense.

EMERGENCY FUNDS

When you start to get organized with your money, I highly recommend setting up a little emergency fund—and make sure that you only use it for emergencies! Ensure that you have enough cash to carry you through things like loss of employment, vet bills, car repairs, etc. You are the only one that can determine what amount of money you should set aside every month. I take about 5 per cent of my net pay and throw it into my savings account as an emergency fund. I've found that number works well for me. But consider your situation and how much money you will need if and when an emergency arises.

An emergency fund should be built along with your savings and investing. One of the keys to successful finances is balance. Balance your spending, saving and investing, emergency funds, and debt reduction.

6
Get Investing, Part I:
THE BASICS

So, you've got the motivation, the goals, and some basic financial fundamentals under your belt. You know how to properly budget and you've identified areas in your budget where you might free up some dollars. Now it's time to get down to the nitty gritty of investing. In this chapter, we're going to cover some investment basics—why to invest, what type of investor you are, what all those strange terms mean. In chapter 7, we'll look specifically at the various investment options and strategies. Hang in for the ride because this information is valuable. It's your ticket to becoming a millionaire.

Why Should I Invest?

What comes to mind when you hear the word "investing"? The most common response invariably has to do with money. For many of us, investing refers to the actions we take when we put money into the market place, a home, a stock, or a bond. But if we broaden our scope a little, we realize that the term can be used to describe many other things. You can invest in your education, for example, or invest your time. At its most basic, investing means that you are building your resources—whatever those may be.

You are an investor right now! You're investing in your education by reading this book. You're also investing your time and energy. And, as with any good investment, your efforts will pay off with increased financial knowledge and better financial health.

Just as investing means different things to different people, people chose to invest for their own personal reasons. I want to invest my money for the future. I also want to invest it for the present. When I think of investing any of my money, I have five primary objectives:

1) **Safety:** I want to invest my money in a way that ensures I won't lose it all.
2) **Income:** I want to use my invested money as income in the future.
3) **Growth:** I want to grow my money using the power of compound interest.
4) **Liquidity:** I want to invest my money in things that are easy to buy and sell.
5) **Tax Minimization:** I want my investments to help minimize the taxes I pay.

If you're scratching your head and wondering what the heck I'm talking about, don't worry. You're about to learn that good investments can meet all of these objectives. For now, I just want you to think about your investment goals. What do you want to achieve?

If you're still scratching your head, try flipping back to chapter 1. In the chart on page 27, you wrote down some of your personal and financial goals. What were your long-term goals? Where do you want to be ten, twenty, or fifty years from now? Do you want to retire at forty-five and sail your yacht around the world? Own a family cottage on the shores of a northern lake? When you're considering your future—specifically, anything more than three years away—you need to shift your financial thinking from short term to long term. And to achieve long-term financial success you must **invest** your money.

Over the long haul, money grows much faster if it is invested rather than simply saved. Investment offers a greater potential for a higher return. History backs me up on this. For the past two hundred years, investments in things like stocks, bonds, and mutual funds have consistently outperformed the lowly savings account. Check out the chart below:

Power of Saving and Investing

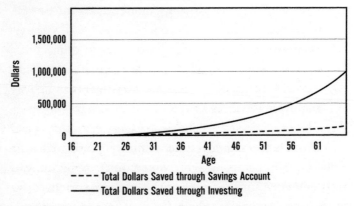

Saving your money is always better than spending it, but investing for the long term is the best idea of all.

The Power of Interest

So how does this work? Investing makes more money than savings over the long haul because of compound interest. We talked about this a bit back in chapter 1, when we were discussing the importance of time. Compound interest is like growing your money for free. You earn interest on your initial investment. That interest is reinvested, and you end up earning interest on it as well. Now, you're earning interest on your interest. How cool is that?

The chart below demonstrates the power of compound interest. If you start investing your money at the age of sixteen, you'll be a millionaire by the time you are sixty-five—and it takes only $35 per month to start! A savings account, on the other hand, will leave you with approximately one-tenth of that million-dollar payout. (The chart assumes an average 8.5 per cent rate of return on the investment and 1 per cent on the savings account. It also assumes that you invest the total dollars saved at the end of the year, rather than in monthly installments. This is for ease of calculation.)

In constructing this chart, I made a few basic assumptions. First, I assumed that the investor would increase the amount invested each month at certain life stages. By twenty-three, for example, it's reasonable to expect that most young people will have a slightly greater earning potential. They are either nearing completion of post-secondary education or they have already started in their career. Perhaps they are just in a job that pays more than it used to. Whatever the reason, by twenty-three, most young people can afford to increase

AGE	$'S SAVED PER MONTH	$'S SAVED PER YEAR	TOTAL $'S SAVED	$'S SAVED WITH SAVINGS INTEREST (1%)	TOTAL $'S SAVED THROUGH INVESTING (8.5%)
16	35	420	420	424.20	455.70
17	35	420	840	852.64	950.13
18	35	420	1,260	1,285.37	1,486.60
19	35	420	1,680	1,722.42	2,068.66
20	35	420	2,100	2,163.85	2,700.19
21	35	420	2,520	2,609.68	3,385.41
22	35	420	2,940	3,059.98	4,128.87
23	150	1800	4,740	4,908.58	6,432.82
24	150	1,800	6,540	6,775.67	8,932.61
25	150	1,800	8,340	8,661.42	11,644.88
26	150	1,800	10,140	10,566.04	14,587.70
27	150	1,800	11,940	12,489.70	17,780.65
28	150	1,800	13,740	14,432.60	21,245.01
29	150	1,800	15,540	16,394.92	25,003.84
30	250	3,000	18,540	19,588.87	30,384.16
31	250	3,000	21,540	22,814.76	36,221.81
32	250	3,000	24,540	26,072.91	42,555.67
33	250	3,000	27,540	29,363.64	49,427.90
34	250	3,000	30,540	32,687.27	56,884.27
35	250	3,000	33,540	36,044.15	64,974.44
36	250	3,000	36,540	39,434.59	73,752.26
37	250	3,000	39,540	42,858.93	83,276.21
38	250	3,000	42,540	46,317.52	93,609.68
39	250	3,000	45,540	49,810.70	104,821.51
40	350	4,200	49,740	54,550.80	118,288.33
41	350	4,200	53,940	59,338.31	132,899.84
42	350	4,200	58,140	64,173.70	148,753.33
43	350	4,200	62,340	69,057.43	165,954.36

AGE	$'S SAVED PER MONTH	$'S SAVED PER YEAR	TOTAL $'S SAVED	$'S SAVED WITH SAVINGS INTEREST (1%)	TOTAL $'S SAVED THROUGH INVESTING (8.5%)
44	350	4,200	66,540	73,990.01	184,617.48
45	350	4,200	70,740	78,971.91	204,866.97
46				79,761.63	222,280.66
47				80,559.24	241,174.52
48				81,364.83	261,674.35
49				82,178.48	283,916.67
50				83,000.27	308,049.59
51				83,830.27	334,233.80
52				84,668.57	362,643.68
53				85,515.26	393,468.39
54				86,370.41	426,913.20
55				87,234.12	463,200.82
56				88,106.46	502,572.89
57				88,987.52	545,291.59
58				89,877.40	591,641.37
59				90,776.17	641,930.89
60				91,683.93	696,495.02
61				92,600.77	755,697.09
62				93,526.78	819,931.35
63				94,462.05	889,625.51
64				95,406.67	965,243.68
65				$96,360.73	$1,047,289.39

their monthly contribution. Additional increases, for similar reasons, happen at thirty and forty. By forty-five, you could theoretically stop investing your money and just sit on it until you retire. If you did this, you'd have approximately $1 million by the time you retired.

These are just assumptions and they don't take into account the unique situations in which you might find yourself. Maybe you'll be in school until you're twenty-eight, or end up earning a lot of money working overseas at age twenty. Whatever your circumstances, the key is to save and invest your money regularly to take advantage of compound interest starting at a young age.

Stick It Out!

Sandra is thirty-five years old. Five years ago, she temporarily lost her job and stopped investing. She didn't have any extra income, and besides, her money wasn't growing as fast as she'd hoped it would anyway. She cashed in her investments, bought a condo and a car, and now, she's kicking herself because she has zero investment money saved for her retirement. Her best friend, who kept her money invested, is watching it grow. Sandra, on the other hand, worries about the future.

Looking at the chart on pages 94–95, one thing becomes obvious. Unlike savings (which can take place over time periods ranging from a few months to a few years), investing is a long-term proposition. You need patience and commitment to stick to your plan. At the beginning, you may get discouraged by what seems to be a lack of progress (it takes a while for that compound interest thing to really kick in!). If you bail, like Sandra, you'll never achieve your financial goals. If you stick with it, however, you'll start to see the results as time passes, and motivation will no longer be a problem!

Can you think of any reasons why investing over the long term might be difficult for you? Are you an impulse shopper? Do you lack the funds needed to invest? Think about it for a moment, and then check out the following tips designed to help keep you on track:

- **Start as soon as possible.** The earlier you start, the more time you will have to grow your money with compound interest and the sooner you'll see results. Also, investing every month will become a habit, making it easier to keep up as time passes.
- **Choose a reasonable amount of money to invest.** Strike a balance between the money you save and the money you invest. There's no point setting your goals too high; if you fail, you'll get discouraged and you might give up. When you create your own budget, think carefully about how much you can afford to set aside. And don't worry if the amount seems small. Even $10 a month is better than nothing!
- **Automate your monthly contribution.** Have your financial institution take your monthly investment contribution straight out of your bank account on the day you get paid. That way you won't be tempted to spend your entire paycheque before you invest. Over time, you'll mentally adjust to not having this money. You won't even miss it!
- **Remind yourself that you're doing well.** While you don't want to obsess over the financial details of your life, it's not a bad idea to check in on your accounts once a month to remind yourself that you are making

progress. Keep a chart on your wall, or set up a spreadsheet on your computer. Being able to visualize your success will help keep you on track.

Now that you're clear on why you should be investing, you can start to think about the types of investments that might work for you. In chapter 7, we'll look carefully at the various investment options available, but before you start throwing money at the hottest stock or trendiest mutual fund, there are a few more things you need to know—starting with yourself!

Investor, Know Thyself!

Would you feed your fish dog food? It's doubtful. If you did, your fish (deprived of the nutrients it needs to survive) would likely end up floating at the top of its tank by the end of the week. Likewise, if you attempted to serve fish flakes to your dog, Fido wouldn't be a happy camper.

A young person's needs and desires are unique. Like the fish and the dog, each of us requires different things to satisfy our various needs. If these needs aren't met, we won't thrive. Our investment needs are no exception.

Unlike savings, which works in pretty much the same way for everyone, investing can be a highly personal undertaking. Before you dive in, it's a good idea to work up an investment plan. And before you can do that, you need to understand both your goals and your investment profile.

Investor Profiles

A happy investor is one whose investment goals and choices are properly aligned—someone who knows the types of investment options that are best going to suit his or her needs and personality. Discovering your investor profile isn't difficult. If you visit a bank with the intention of setting up an investment account, they'll likely present you with a long, drawn-out questionnaire, or ask you about a hundred questions—all designed to tell them what type of investment options would best suit your needs. Below are some of the most common questions. If you answer them honestly, you'll have a pretty good sense of your own investment profile.

WHAT ARE YOUR PERSONAL GOALS? Well! It's lucky we've already answered this one, isn't it? Refer back to chapter 1 and the discussion on goal setting. The goals you wrote down on page 27 will work just fine as an answer to this question.

WHAT IS YOUR INVESTMENT TIME HORIZON? This question is very important. Not all goals can be achieved with the same investment strategies. Take, for example, Rachel—a high school student who is desperately trying to save for college. Let's say that Rachel doesn't have access to student loans. Because she needs this money within a few years, and she can't afford to lose any of it, Rachel needs to put her money into a safe investment—one that won't lose value in the short term.

Someone with a longer investment time horizon, however, would have more time during which to make up losses and enjoy gains. This person's strategy would be very different from Rachel's.

WHERE WILL YOUR MONEY BE COMING FROM? Money from a regular income is different than money given to an individual on a one-time basis. This can affect the type of investment you choose. Kyle, for example, works on commission and gets paid every three months. If you're in a similar situation, your cash flow is going to be different from someone working a regular hourly wage job. Also, commission is temperamental and can vary from time to time. Because Kyle's cash flow is all over the map, it's important for him to work out a reasonable investment plan that fits his money schedule.

DO YOU HAVE ANY TAX OR LEGAL CONCERNS? Many investors want to take advantage of tax considerations that will allow them to pay less personal income tax. If this is one of your investment goals, there are a number of investments on the market that can assist.

WHAT ROLE DO YOU WANT TO PLAY WHEN IT COMES TO YOUR MONEY? Informing your investment adviser about how involved you want to be with your money will ensure that they understand some of your needs. Your involvement will affect the choices you make and the workload your adviser has to do.

WHAT IS YOUR RISK TOLERANCE? This is the big one—the most important question of all when it comes to determining your investment profile. Risk tolerance is a vital piece of the investment puzzle. To invest without going insane, you need to match your risk tolerance to your needs. If you don't like the idea of investments that change in value from day to day, you may not want to participate in the stock market. On the other hand, if you've got a stomach for handling the ups and downs of the market, you may want to take advantage of risky investments so that you can benefit from a higher reward in the long run. You can have some fun with the following quiz to see what type of investor you are:

1) When your math teacher comes walking up to you with a grim "you're in trouble" look on her face you:
    a) listen as she accuses you of something that you didn't do. You don't like confrontation and so you choose not to correct her.
    b) say, "I'm not exactly sure what the problem is. Can you explain what's happened?" You then listen carefully to what she has to say.
    c) deny, deny, deny.

2) Some kids down the street received new cars for their birthdays. They want to race against your dad's new sports car—a car you're normally not allowed to go near. You:
    a) grab the keys to the shiny red roadster and kick off the neighbourhood Indy 500 in style.
    b) walk away from these bullies without giving them an answer.
    c) tell them your dad's car is worth more than all of theirs put together and that you'd rather eat dirt than face your father's wrath when he finds you with the keys in your hot little hands.

3) You're in a store where an attractive sales assistant works. She (or he) approaches you and asks if you need any help. You:
    a) tell her you're looking for a pair of pants and say that you really like her outfit. Hey, if you find

some equally trendy clothes, maybe she'll ask for your number!

b) turn beet red and say, "Thanks, but I can find my own clothes."

c) say, "Sure, you can help me" and ask for her number when you're leaving.

4) If you were given $1000 for doing a great job at the local science fair, what would you likely spend your money on?

a) spend $400 on some new clothing. Save $500 in your investment account and donate $100 back to the science fair committee.

b) take your closest friends out for a day of snowboarding and eating nachos. The cost of your trip would be $1000.

c) stuff it *all* away under your mattress or in your piggy bank.

5) You buy a new condominium with your hard-earned money at the age of twenty-one. You've got a reasonable mortgage ($800 per month), a great interest rate, and a roommate that pays $400 each month in rent. If you had an extra $300 a month after all your expenses, fun and necessities were handled, you would:

a) pool your extra money with a friend and buy another condominium that you could rent out.

b) pay down your existing mortgage as fast as possible (you don't like to be in debt).

c) use half the money to fix up your condo (adding value) and put the other half toward your mutual fund investments.

Okay. Now tally your points according to the following:

1. a) 1 point   b) 2 points   c) 3 points
2. a) 3 points   b) 1 point   c) 2 points
3. a) 2 points   b) 1 point   c) 3 points
4. a) 2 points   b) 3 points   c) 1 points
5. a) 3 points   b) 1 point   c) 2 points

If you scored between 5 and 6 points, you're a **non-risky investor**. Your stomach will turn if you are forced into a situation outside your comfort zone. You probably aren't a huge risk taker. For example, you won't likely go cliff diving or willingly give a speech in human health class. Investing money in risky things that aren't guaranteed will not be part of your agenda. The benefit of being a non-risky investor is that you'll be very careful when you choose your *secure* investment vehicles. When the markets get rocky, you won't lose very much money. However, you won't make as much as your riskier counterparts over the long run.

If you scored between 7 and 11 points you're a **moderate investor**. The decisions you make aren't totally wild and off the wall. They tend to be carefully planned and considered. You might be willing to venture out of your comfort zone with your investment choices, but only if they won't endanger your long-term goals. Medium-risk investments are a great fit for you because they earn a higher return than low-risk investments with only a slightly higher risk of loss. However, you're a person that can take loss fairly well. You wouldn't like it, but you'd pick up the pieces and make something new.

MAKING SENSE OF IT ALL

Grab a newspaper and turn to the financial section. Are your eyes glazing over yet? At first glance, it looks incredibly boring. But it isn't. The first column tells you the name of the investment. The second tells you the volume traded that day. The third and fourth columns indicate the highest and lowest price during that particular trading day. The closing price and the change from the previous day's price rounds things out. If you want things to start making sense, pick one stock from the stock market page and follow it daily for the next two weeks. You'll get the hang of it faster than you think!

If you scored between 12 and 15 points, you're a fairly **risky investor** and risky investment choices will suit your personality. You have the potential to make a lot of money when times are good, and to lose a lot of money when times are bad—if you don't protect yourself. If you're going to follow the risky-investor route, do so with a little bit of caution. Include some safer choices in your mix as well, and remember, there are some investment options that even professionals won't touch!

An Investment Primer: Talking the Talk

You're almost there. You're almost ready to take the plunge. There's only one more thing you need to know. Okay... it's more than one thing. It's several things. Dozens maybe. As you read this chapter and the next, you're going to come across a lot of weird and wacky words that you may not have seen before (you may have already encountered a few that you don't fully understand). Before we start talking about bonds and GICs and RESPs and the like (which will be defined in the next chapter), let's wrap our heads around some investing lingo:

- **Investment option or vehicle:** Anything (like a mutual fund, stock, bond, or Treasury bill, to name a few) into which you can invest your money.
- **Investment portfolio:** Your personal combination of investment options. A portfolio is geared specifically to your needs and investment style. It can be risky, moderate- or low-risk.
- **Market:** A place where buyers and sellers meet to trade things of value. We buy and sell investments. Newspapers list the market prices for these items on those pages with all the tiny little numbers. There are two major stock markets in North America: the New York Stock Exchange and the Toronto Stock Exchange. There are also mutual fund markets, money markets, bond markets, and more.
- **Market cycles:** Financial markets tend to experience cycles. Sometimes they perform well, sometimes poorly. This tends to happen in waves. When the markets are performing poorly, the economy is slow. The opposite is also true. The five most common market cycles are:
    - **Expansion:** An upwards trend. New businesses and jobs are being created and people are investing more money in the market place. The economy is growing and inflation is stable. This is

a good time to be purchasing investments because they will grow in value throughout this cycle.

- **Peak:** Labour shortages start, wages increase significantly, demand for product is high, and interest rates are very high. Because prices have increased significantly, the market begins to react negatively. Investments like stocks and bonds tend to be very expensive. This isn't a good time to be purchasing investments, homes, cars, or other big-ticket items. They are overpriced and can lose value in the next cycle.

- **Recession or Contraction:** Economic activity begins to slow down. Unemployment rates start to rise and there is less money available in the market place. Typically, it is a difficult time for people to save or invest any money whatsoever.

- **Trough:** The lowest part of the business cycle. Prices have fallen substantially and so have interest rates. Consumers tend to be short on cash, but because of low interest rates, they are able to borrow money and purchase items like homes and investments at lower prices. This is the best time to purchase investments because they can be very undervalued.

- **Recovery:** An expansionary cycle during which the market starts to return to its previous peak. Many big-ticket items are purchased throughout this time and because of the increase in demand prices start to increase again. This is a good time to be purchasing investments because the prices are still relatively low.

Markets change from year to year. Overall, however, the stock and mutual fund markets in North America have survived the ups and downs and provided an average return between 11 per cent and 13 per cent. Not bad. The ups and downs of the market (especially the stock market) are also referred to as the "bull" or "bear" markets. When we experience a bull market, the average price of stocks, bonds, and mutual funds tends to increase. During a bear market, prices decrease.

Now that you know some of the basics, it's time to start putting the pieces of this investment puzzle together. In the next chapter, we will talk about building your own investment portfolio. This is the exciting part!

7

Get Investing, Part II:

OPTIONS AND STRATEGIES

In the previous chapter, you learned more about what investing is, why you should do it and what type of investor you are. This knowledge is a powerful tool that will help you become a successful investor. In this chapter, we're going to get into some of the specific investment options and strategies that are open to you. This is the fun part!

Investment Options

A few years ago, I was teaching a "Dollars and Sense" course to an eighth-grade class. Throughout my presentation, I used the term **investment vehicle** a number of times. Near the end of the session, I asked the class to draw a picture or write a paragraph about what they had learned throughout the day. I reviewed their work that evening and discovered a number of pictures of cars—cars on roads, cars in driveways, cars on top of mountains. Clearly, something had gotten lost in translation!

An investment vehicle is any type of investment that you use to grow your money. Your investment portfolio is made up of a number of different investment vehicles. Some investment vehicles can even hold other vehicles— kind of like a car carrier! We'll get to the details about that in a few pages, but right now, let's take a look at the investment vehicles, or options, that are available to you. Knowing what they are and how they work will help you decide what options are best for you.

Investment Options

INVESTMENT TYPE	DESCRIPTION
Savings Account	A savings account is a regular bank account where you can keep your money. In general, savings accounts pay very little interest and are easy to access—a drawback when trying to save for the long term.
Stock	A stock is a certificate that indicates ownership in a company. If the company is doing well, the value of your stock increases. If the company is doing not-so-well, the value of your stock will likely decrease.
Bond	A bond is a certificate indicating that a company, an association, or a government has borrowed money from you. In return for making your funds available, the bond issuer will pay you a fixed amount of interest after a fixed period of time. Rates of return on bonds fluctuate with interest rates.

Treasury Bills (T-Bills)	A treasury bill is issued when a government borrows money from you and promises to pay it back, usually within one year. You do not gain interest on the money that you lend the government. The bill is sold to you at a discounted rate, and purchased back at full value.
Guaranteed Investment Certificate (GIC)	A GIC is similar to a savings account, in that it's a very safe investment vehicle (you're guaranteed to get all of your money back), but unlike savings accounts, you earn a decent rate of return. Your money is locked away for a period of time ranging from thirty days up to ten years. Interest can either be paid or compounded.
Mutual Funds	A mutual fund is a professionally managed investment vehicle that pools money from many individuals and invests it according to a common objective. It refers to a group of stocks. You buy units of the group, allowing you to own a little bit of many stocks. Although not guaranteed to make you money, they do provide a great opportunity to diversify your portfolio.
Index Funds	An index fund is a group of stocks pulled together to represent a specific part of the market—such as the S&P 500. Money invested is not guaranteed, although the opportunity to diversify is high.

Savings Account

A savings account can be a good place to keep your money, but only *in the short term*. Savings accounts are considered to be "liquid" investment opportunities, which means that it's easy to get your hands on your cash. This is fine if you're using the account to store cash for things like groceries or rent, but it's not so good if you actually want to prevent yourself from spending! Also on the plus side? Because you are effectively loaning the bank your money (they invest it, after all; it doesn't just sit there in the vault!), they pay you a small—very small!—amount of interest.

Perhaps the best thing about a savings account is that it is a very safe place to keep your money. In Canada, the Canadian Deposit Insurance Corporation (CDIC) will insure a savings account for up to $60,000 in the event of loss or damage. So, unlike some of the other options we're going to discuss, your money is never really at risk.

Stocks

When you purchase stock, you are actually buying a piece of a corporation. You become a shareholder in that company—and you do so with the hope that the value of the corporation will increase, thereby increasing the value of your stock.

There are several ways you can make money on the stock market. You can sell your shares at a higher price than what you paid for them, you can receive a dividend (a payout to shareholders) from the corporation, or you can purchase more stock if and when the company decides to issue a new batch.

The prices of shares in companies vary widely. Some sell for as little as 50 cents (or lower), while others go for $120 (or higher). Because you need to buy stocks through some type of financial institution or brokerage, all come with a transaction fee attached. Also, unlike your average savings account, the money that you invest in stocks is never guaranteed, nor are you guaranteed any dividend payout.

Before you purchase any stock, do your research. Many people lose money on the stock market because they have absolutely no information about the company in which they are investing. Others lose money because they've received a "hot tip" from a friend who may or may not know what they are talking about. Be smart, and dig around a bit. A corporation's risk level can be determined by looking into their history and by examining the direction in which the company is heading. Read the financial section of your newspaper. Go online and poke around the various investment sites.

If you know how to read a financial statement, you'll be able to assess a company's value potential. If you don't, consider consulting a financial adviser. One key thing you'll want to know is whether or not the company can afford to pay its short- and long-term debts. You can figure this out by dividing the company's current assets by its current liabilities. If the end result is a figure less than 1.2, the company may be in a bit of trouble in the short term. Another trick is to calculate a debt-to-equity ratio (divide total liabilities by total equity) to see if the company can afford to pay their debts in the long term. If the number produced is greater than 2 or 3, the company may not be able to afford their debt payments over time.

Whatever you decide to do, make sure you approach stock-market investing with your eyes wide open. Even with ample research, it's possible to lose money on the stock market. Without investing, however, you're at an even greater disadvantage.

Why? The stock market has typically performed better than any other type of investment in the long run. Since 1970, the stock market (measured by the Standard & Poor's 500) has increased nearly 200 per cent. The rate of return calculated by the S&P 500 index has been between 11 per cent and 13 per cent over the years. Savings rates tend to be much lower, like 1.5 to 3 per cent. Let's assume that you invested $1,000 in 1970 in a diversified stock market portfolio. If you gained that 200 per cent average, your $1,000 then would be worth nearly $200,000 today.

If you take the time to understand how it works and what stocks are best for you, you can certainly do well over time.

Bonds

When a company or a government needs more money than it currently has, it may look to investors (like you!) for financial support. By issuing bonds, the company or government can find the capital it needs to stay in business. A bond states that the borrower will pay a certain rate of return (interest rate) over the next few years or until the bond matures.

A bond makes investors money through the payment of interest. Some companies will issue a cheque every quarter (three months) to the investor for the amount of interest they have gained throughout that period. The amount varies depending on the amount of the bond and how many bonds the investor has. Other types of bonds don't issue interest cheques at all. Instead, they wait until the bond matures. At that point, they pay back both the principal amount and the compounded interest.

When you purchase a bond, the issuer presents you with a certificate stating the name of the company or government, the dollar amount invested, the interest rate promised, and the maturity date. In Canada, you must be eighteen years old to buy a bond through a broker, bank, or other financial institution. Under the age of eighteen, you will need a parent or guardian to approve the transaction.

There are two main types of bonds: government and corporate.

- **Government bonds** tend to have secure rates of return and are sold in minimum denominations of $100. The maturity date is stated at the time of purchase, although the investor can usually cash in the bond prior to that date. A choice between compound or simple interest is often available. If you have the choice, take compound interest—it will make a big difference to the overall value of your portfolio.
- **Corporate bonds** are almost identical to government bonds, although you'll likely need to put up more money to buy one. Bonds are generally considered a "safer" investment vehicle than stocks. Why? A bond is a corporation's *written legal promise* that it will repay a specified amount of money with interest after a specified amount of time. If the company happens to go bankrupt during that time, they are legally required to pay back anyone with a claim to the com-

pany's assets. No such promise exists with shareholders and stocks.

Although bonds are considered safe, there's a downside to consider as well. The rate of return on a bond can be less than the rate of return you might receive on other investment vehicles—like mutual funds, registered investments, stocks, and securities. However, if a corporation that has a risky financial situation issues bonds, they often have to pay a higher rate of return to their investors. There is a tradeoff between risk and reward. As a general rule of thumb, less risky investment vehicles pay lower rates of return whereas more risky investments pay a higher return.

Bonds are best used as long-term investments. Maturity dates tend to be anywhere from five to thirty years after the date of issue. When the maturity date arrives, the bond will no longer earn interest. It is ready to be cashed by the investor or reinvested. If you want to cash your bond in early, there may be a penalty.

As with the stock market, you need to do your research before you buy. All bonds have a rating. The rating system looks like this:

RATING	MEANING
AAA	High Credit Quality (Best Ones)
AA	Very Good Quality
A	Good Quality
BBB	Medium Quality
BB	Low–Medium Quality
B	Poor Quality
CCC	Sketchy Quality (Could miss payments)
CC	Very Sketchy Quality (Usually misses payments)

C	Extremely Sketchy Quality (Bankruptcy has been filed)
D	Default (The company is being forced to liquidate)
	Suspended Rating (Serious financial trouble)

Clearly, bonds with a CCC rating are considered a more risky investment than bonds with an AAA rating. Taking this into account, a CCC-rated bond would likely feature a very attractive rate of return. However, if the issuing company slips into a D rating, you have to wait until the legal battles are settled before you get your money back. Even then, you might not receive all that you invested. Be smart. Invest according to your risk tolerance.

Treasury Bills (T-Bills)

Unlike bonds, treasury bills are short-term investments, geared toward people who want to invest their money for ninety to 120 days. A treasury bill is issued when a government borrows money from you and promises to pay you back, usually within one year. Unlike with a bond, you do not gain interest on the money you lend. Rather, you lend your money at a discount and the government "tops you up" when the money is due to be returned. For example, you might buy a T-bill for $9,500 that is worth $10,000 on its maturity date. On the date of maturity you are paid $10,000. Typically you cannot get your money out of the T-bill until its maturity date.

The T-bill usually requires a large sum of money to invest—between $5,000 and $10,000 to start—making it an ideal place to stash cash for big-ticket items like cars, vacations or down payments. The returns are moderate, but so is the risk. A T-bill can be purchased through a broker, bank, or other financial institution. If you are under eighteen, a legal parent or guardian is needed to sign off on this purchase.

Guaranteed Investment Certificates

A Guaranteed Investment Certificate (GIC) is another good low-risk investment. Issued by the bank, GICs can be purchased for a minimum investment of $500 (although some institutions allow you to buy in via weekly or monthly plans for as little as $25 to $35 per month). The maturity terms can be anywhere from a few months to ten or fifteen years. As with bonds and T-bills, the rate of return on a GIC is higher than what a savings account would offer, but lower than many other types of investments. However, the tradeoff is also the same: it's a less risky investment. In Canada, you can buy into a GIC through a bank at the age of twelve (although you may need an adult's permission).

One of the catches with GICs is that your money is "locked in" until the maturity date (if you want it back earlier, there can be a penalty). Although some consider it a drawback, this feature actually makes the GIC an excellent tool for individuals who are easily tempted to spend their money. It's also an ideal vehicle for investors hoping to make a big-ticket purchase within a few years.

Because the GIC pays a relatively low interest rate, a young investor likely wouldn't want to keep all their money in GICs for the long term. Over the long run, stocks, bonds, and mutual funds will outperform a GIC.

Mutual Funds

Back on page 109, we talked about investment vehicles that contain other vehicles. That's a perfect description of a mutual fund. Another analogy that often works is that of an umbrella: the mutual fund is the umbrella, under which are gathered a number of diverse stock investments.

A mutual fund is a group of stocks (or, in some situations, bonds) that a portfolio manager has chosen and crammed into a unit. The manager chooses the stocks with their clients' best interests in mind, and the stocks are generally similar in terms of their risk factor. When you buy one unit of a mutual fund, you are actually buying a little bit of every stock within that unit. It is a wonderful tool for investors looking to diversify and balance their portfolios.

A mutual fund has a greater potential to make money than T-bills, bonds, and GICs, but there is also more risk involved. Because you are dealing with the stock market, you are indirectly subject to its volatility. Mutual funds follow the market cycles very closely. When the markets are generally in a slump, your mutual funds are likely going to be worth less. When the markets are hot, your funds will be too.

Mutual funds are categorized according to goals and risk levels. For example, a low-risk mutual fund would hold a grouping of low-risk stocks. There are growth funds (featuring higher risk, higher return investments), aggressive-growth funds, international funds, income-producing funds, and many more.

The mutual-fund market offers a wonderful opportunity for new investors. Unlike some other investment vehicles, mutual funds are cheap! While you may not be able to afford a significant quantity of stock, or a T-bill, you can invest in the stock market through mutual funds for as little as $50 per month. Think about that for a minute. Fifty dollars a month equals two dinners out with friends. Not a big investment, and a potentially high rate of return!

Mutual funds are best used as long-term investments. Ideally, investing in mutual funds until retirement gives you ample time to grow them. However, the shortest of the long-term time frame is likely closer to ten years. To receive the full benefit of a high rate of return, you must stick with your fund whether the markets are good or bad. If you hop from mutual fund to mutual fund, you end up missing out on their long-term growth potential.

MUTUAL FUND FEES

Mutual fund managers are paid a yearly management fee. Usually, this is out of the fund itself, not your portfolio directly. The management fee is often a percentage of the earnings that the fund makes throughout the year. It can be anywhere between 0.5 and 4 per cent. Although some investors grumble about these fees, many others consider it a necessary expense. You are, in essence, paying for a service. Your fund manager is well educated and informed— just the kind of person to help you make good investment decisions.

Index Funds

Somewhat like mutual funds in terms of their umbrella quality, index funds (also called **exchange traded funds**) allow you to buy a small piece of a large number of companies in the same industry or market. Index funds include ones that track the major indexes (like the Dow Jones, or S&P 500) as well as ones that follow specific sectors (finance, technology, health). In Canada, there are 178 index funds and eighteen exchange traded funds (according to 2006 data) which can be purchased through almost any financial institution. You can also purchase them through your own self-managed investment account. Unlike mutual funds, index funds are usually managed by a computer and therefore have very limited management fees.

Although index funds have been around for a long while, they are still relatively underused. But that shouldn't scare you off. These investment vehicles are great for new investors. They're affordable, they allow for diversification within an industry, and they're not as risky as investing in stocks alone. One of the very best things about investing in index funds is that you'll never under-perform the market (which averages between 10 and 13 per cent). This is because your fund is a representation *of* the market. If there's one disadvantage it's that you'll never outperform the market either.

A good strategy when purchasing index funds is to look for industries (sectors) that are trending upwards. For example, over the past few decades, the banking and financial services industry has consistently done well. To succeed with sector funds, it is important to catch the trends and ride them like you would if you were surfing on a wave. When one sector starts to slow, catch the next trend and ride it. To do this successfully, you need to keep current with what is going on in various industries. Beef up your business knowledge. It will pay off in the long run.

Investment Strategies

Now that you know what's available to you, and a little bit about how to use it, actually building your investment portfolio is the next step to financial success. In the pages that follow you'll be introduced to some key investing strategies.

Many of the strategies presented here are not "get rich quick" schemes. Instead, they are based on sound investment advice that will carry you comfortably into your future. Sometimes you'll make money fast, other times the growth will be slower. But ultimately these are proven and successful long-term strategies.

Diversify and Balance

"Don't put all your eggs in one basket!" We've all heard this one before, haven't we? In terms of investing, this phrase cautions against putting all of your money in one place. After all, if you lose that one basket, you've lost everything in it! However, if you diversify, the loss of one basket along the way won't be quite so devastating.

Another way to think about this is in terms of balance. That word—"balance"—will be a huge part of your financial life forever. It is crucial to success in investing (not to mention in your personal life!). Financially successful people learn how to balance spending, saving, investing, and giving back. In chapter 6, we looked at how important it is to create a portfolio that is well suited to your investment personality. But even the most well defined investors need to balance. Let's look at a few examples.

Amy is comfortable taking risks. As an eighteen-year-old student with plenty of support from her mom and dad, she knows she can afford to go after high-risk, high-yield investments. Amy has saved up her income from the past three summers and has about $6,000 to invest. After lots of research and discussion with her parents, however, Amy knows that she shouldn't risk everything. She wants to have some portion of her money in secure investments just in case her aggressive/risky strategy takes a turn for the worst. So, she consults with a financial adviser at her local bank. After she shares her financial goals, they determine that she would benefit most from a combination of growth-oriented investments and more conservative, non-risky investments. In the end, Amy's investment portfolio looks like this:

Amy's Portfolio for Aggressive Growth

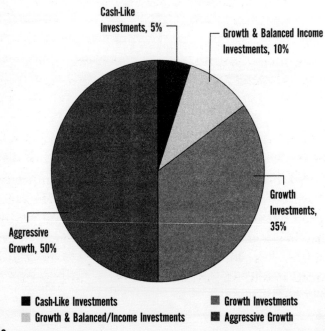

Cash-Like Investments, 5%

Growth & Balanced Income Investments, 10%

Growth Investments, 35%

Aggressive Growth, 50%

■ Cash-Like Investments   ▦ Growth Investments
▦ Growth & Balanced/Income Investments   ■ Aggressive Growth

Let me take a moment to explain the labels that appear on this graph. You're going to see them throughout this chapter. Simply put, they describe a few of the investment types available for Amy's needs.

- **Cash-Like Investments:** These investments are very secure and very liquid (you can get your money out easily). Example: a savings account or T-bill.
- **Growth and Balanced Income Investments:** These investments are a little more risky. They typically don't yield a huge return, yet they provide security. Example: a low-risk mutual fund or low-risk stocks in very reputable companies.
- **Growth Investments:** These are riskier yet. They will provide a higher yield and will have a more aggressive approach to making money. Example: a growth-oriented mutual fund, index fund, or stock in a company that is secure but is in growth or expansion mode.
- **Aggressive Growth:** High risk/high reward investments. Example: hot stocks or high-risk mutual funds.

But what if you're not like Amy? What if all that risk makes you a little nervous? Juan, for example, knows that he needs to be super careful with the $3,500 he's managed to save as he heads into university and beyond. He wants a good rate of return, but he simply can't afford to risk what he's managed to save so far. Based on his own research, he's decided to construct a portfolio based around mostly safe investment vehicles. Juan's portfolio looks like this:

Juan's Portfolio for Conservative Growth

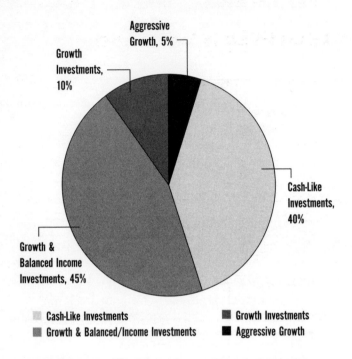

Most investors will likely fall somewhere between Amy and Juan on the risk scale. And that's just fine. Whatever your desired rate of return, you can combine your types of investments so that they can give you that kind of return. Let's look at one more example.

Twenty-six-year-old Andrea has some money to invest, but she isn't sure that she wants a whole lot of risk. After talking to an adviser at the bank, she decided to take advantage of her youth and her ability to weather the market. Based on her adviser's recommendation, Andrea knows that she'd like to earn a return of between 8 and 10 per cent over the long run—what investors typically call "balanced growth." Andrea's portfolio might look something like the this:

Andrea's Portfolio for Balanced Growth

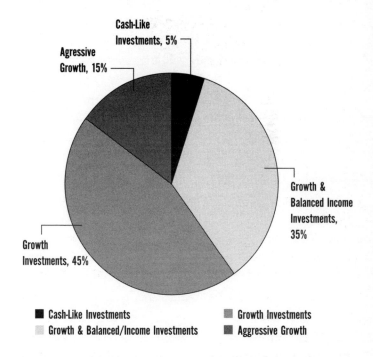

Whatever *your* combination, your ultimate goal is to have an investment bundle that meets your needs. Like Amy, you might be willing to tolerate a certain amount of risk. Or perhaps you're more conservative, like Juan. Chances are good that a fair number of you will fall into Andrea territory—ready to invest but not ready to risk it all. Talk to an adviser at your local bank. Take Andrea's sample portfolio with you. Don't be afraid to ask questions—even ones that you think sound dumb. You have enough knowledge now to ensure that you get what you need out of the various investment options available to you. Use it!

Dollar Cost Averaging

Once you've got the diversification and balance thing down, and you've chosen the investment vehicles that are right for you, you can start thinking about how to maximize your investment dollars. Dollar cost averaging is one really neat trick. Simply defined, it means making a contribution to some type of investment plan on a regular basis. For example, you may contribute $30 a month from your job earnings or your allowance. Over time, you buy $30 each month of that investment, say it's a mutual fund. Due to changes in the market, the cost of that mutual fund fluctuates—sometimes the cost may be low, sometimes it may be higher. By purchasing regularly, you are taking advantage of the fund's average cost, buying more units when the cost is low, and less when the cost is high. And regardless of the cost, you still experience the benefits of compounded interest.

Some investors think that saving up and contributing one lump sum of money will be the best way to invest. They often wait around for the prices of their desired investments to decrease so that they are cheaper to buy. All the while, they are missing out on the advantages of being in the market the entire time. It is hard to time the market. You don't want to be waiting around with thousands of dollars to invest, earning zero interest on the sum.

Dollar cost averaging allows investors to be in the market at all times, taking advantage of both its highs and lows. Here's how it works. Let's say that Jason is investing in a mutual fund called xyz. The average monthly prices are listed in the chart below. If Jason invests once per month, his average cost of buying the mutual fund is $55.91:

MONTH	PRICE
January	$50.25
February	$52.36
March	$60.13
April	$55.12
May	$61.11
June	$60.01
July	$57.63
August	$55.68
September	$54.89
October	$54.23
November	$55.62
December	$53.89
Average Price	**$55.91**

If Jason tried to time the market and hold onto his investment dollars until he thought the time was right, he might end up paying more or less than this average. Perhaps he'd decide, after watching xyz drop in value between May and July, that it wasn't going to go any lower. Not only would he be wrong, but he'd end up paying more than the average cost over a year. Investing regularly makes sense.

Always Take Free Money

If you're working at a full-time job, you may have access to a compensation plan that includes retirement savings. Often, these plans allow you to contribute a certain percentage of your pay (taken straight off your paycheque) to the plan. Your employer would then contribute up to the same amount. Let's say your company agrees to match your contribution, up to $50 a month. If you contribute $50, an additional $50 will be deposited into your savings plan (if you put in $40, your employer will put in $40. If you put in $60, your employer will put in $50). Your employer may not double your contribution, but free money is free money. Take it! Even better, both your money and the money your employer has contributed will earn interest. Short of winning the lottery, it doesn't get any better than that!

Here are a few types of investment vehicles and plans that you should ask about when you start working:

- **Registered Retirement Savings Plans** (RRSPs): RRSPs allow you to group different investment options together into one plan. An RRSP could include some stocks, some mutual funds, and a bond or two. These plans allow you to save money for your retirement. The government will allow you to deduct most, if not all, of what you save from your taxable income. (See chapter 8 for more information.)
- **Registered Education Savings Plans** (RESPs): Like RRSPs, RESPs allow you to group investment options together into one plan. In this instance, however, the goal is to save for your child's education. The government will contribute 20 per cent of your contribution up to a total of $800 a year.

Prepare for the Long Haul (or Don't Buy High and Sell Low)

Looking down the road of life, what does "the long haul" mean to you? Fifty years? Forty? Thirty-five? It's worth thinking about for a moment. Here's why.

Over the past century, the mutual-fund and stock markets have averaged a return of 11 to 13 per cent. Many investors, however, don't reap the benefits of that excellent rate of return. Instead, they average a mere 4 per cent. Why? Investors earning 4 per cent are those who keep changing and shuffling their portfolio. When the market environment changes, they get scared—buying new investment options, selling old ones. Regardless of what they're doing, they're usually doing it at precisely the wrong time, probably because they're letting their emotions prevail.

Those emotions work like this. When the markets are performing poorly, the overall value of your portfolio tends to decrease. In response, you might find yourself getting a little antsy and nervous—after all, you're not making money; you may even be losing money! So what do you do? Well, you might pull money out of your investments, thinking that you'll save yourself from further losses. Actually, you're pulling out when you'll get the least amount of money for your investments. Making matters worse, you might decide to reinvest when the markets take a turn back up. Now, however, the price of investing has increased and you'll be paying more than you should!

This emotional reaction is the complete opposite of a profitable strategy. You're buying high and selling low. If you keep doing this, you won't be making anywhere near that 11 to 13 per cent I mentioned above. You'll be right around the 4 per cent mark instead, which barely beats the rate of inflation.

If you find yourself tempted to tamper, remember this key piece of investment knowledge: to make money with investments, you must leave your money in place for the long haul. Avoid tampering. Tampering costs you money! When your investment statements arrive, look at them quickly and then put them aside. You can examine them in more detail once a year, but you shouldn't need to do it more often than that. A lot can happen in a year and changes may cause you to change your investment strategy. For example, if you had a baby or got married or bought a house, you might want to review your investments/strategies.

Markets change and so do trends. Markets go up and down depending on a number of factors. But you have to ride the ups and downs like everyone else. Ensure that you review your strategies and keep in mind that investing for financial success is a long-term process.

Dividend Strategies

In my final year of university, one of my class groups developed a dividend signalling strategy as part of a course project. We started with the assumption that a corporation's dividend policy has significant signalling implications. Some investors use dividend signalling as a way to analyze the overall health of a company. There is a substantial amount of evidence suggesting that an increase in dividends is viewed positively by the market, while a decrease is understood to be a negative signal. After all, when a company sends out a dividend, it's indicating that it has the money to do so. A dividend reduction sends the opposite message: perhaps this company is in need of cash.

We wanted our mock portfolio to produce positive returns based on dividend signals.

Our strategy was to buy shares in companies that increased their dividend amounts. We held our position in firms with a stable dividend. We sold a portion of our position when firms decreased their dividend amount. Overall, our sample portfolio of forty-six American companies, paying regular dividends, outperformed the benchmark. We even ran the portfolio through recessionary trends in the early part of this decade (the Technology Bubble). Throughout the five-year period over which we tracked our strategy, our average rate of return per year was 14.44 per cent. Our benchmark return was negative through most of those same five years. We were making money and others were not.

Although the implementation of this strategy requires a lot of research, much purchasing and selling of stocks, and a significant amount of money to cover transaction fees, it is nevertheless a lower-risk, stable, and fruitful investment opportunity. If you are interested in giving it a try, you might consider buying into a dividend mutual fund (almost every institution that sells mutual funds has one).

Be Willing to Leverage

If you had enough money available to purchase a big-ticket item, would you use it? Of course, right? Wrong. Some people actually take out loans for certain items even when the necessary money is available. And no, those people are not crazy. Sometimes, borrowing money to make money makes sense. It's called leveraging.

Let's say that you've saved up $5,000 for the purchase of your first used car. You've even found a really great deal on a car with all of the features that you wanted. You figure you'll just pay for the car outright, but when you go to the bank to get a certified cheque, your personal banker tells you about a combination of mutual funds that are expected to earn 10.5 per cent over a three-year period. She tries to convince you that you should invest your $5,000 in this portfolio, rather than putting it all down on the car.

Now you're torn! You want to buy the car, but earning 10.5 per cent on your $5,000 sounds pretty good, too. Luckily, your banker tells you that, through the use of leverage, you can do both. The bank is willing to lend you the $5,000 you need to buy your car at a reasonable interest rate of 7 per cent. You'll have three years to pay back the loan. At the same time, she'll invest the $5,000 you've already saved in the mutual fund portfolio that's expected to earn 10.5 per cent. Because you're earning a higher rate of return than you'll be spending on interest, you're actually making money. In fact, your relative overall rate of return after the three-year period is 3.5 per cent (10.5 minus 7).

Are you interested in knowing how much profit you actually make if everything goes according to plan? (Remember, it's not a straight calculation of interest on the principal amount invested, because interest would be compounded annually.) A handy calculation called the "future value formula" will show you: $P \times (1 + i)^n$. P is principal invested; i is interest rate; and n is investment period: principal multiplied by one plus the interest rate to the exponent of time. If you're head is already pounding, don't worry. This is actually a pretty simple formula that you can plug into any spreadsheet. You don't have to do it in your head!

In the case of you and your car/mutual funds, this is what you need to know: the principal amount invested is

$5,000. The interest rate is 3.5 per cent (in the world of formulas, you have to write this as 0.035 because it is a small part of one whole). The length of time over which the money is being invested is three years. In other words:

$$\$5{,}000 \times (1 + 0.035)^3 = \$5{,}543.59$$

To discover how much money you actually made using this leveraging technique, just subtract the $5,000 that you borrowed from the number above. The grand total is $543.59. Not bad. (If you want to get really fancy, why not consider adding a regular monthly contribution to your initial sum. You'll end up growing your money even more!)

There's one thing to watch out for when using the leverage technique. You do have to make monthly payments on the borrowed money. In the example above, you'd likely be paying close to $150 a month toward your loan. If you can afford to do this, you'll make some decent money a few years down the road.

Call in the Dogs

The Dogs of the Dow strategy was formulated in 1972. Since then, it has proven to be very profitable for those that have followed it. The basic idea is that you purchase your investments when the prices are low and sell them when the prices are high. Makes sense, right? The strategy is implemented by purchasing approximately ten stocks from the exchange. The stocks you buy are the ones with the highest dividend yield at the beginning of the year. These will likely be low in price (hence the term "dogs") because the payment of a dividend decreases the amount of cash available

KNOW YOUR LIMIT

A good financial strategy needs to take your personal limits into account. It is important to know when and if you have made enough (or lost enough) money. You will need to set your own personal standard so that you can be satisfied with your portfolio of investments. For example, perhaps a 20 per cent return works for you. If you're fortunate enough to make a 20 per cent return on a stock or another investment, you'll be ready to sell. Or perhaps you'll set your loss limit at 20 per cent. It's possible that you'll want to alter your personal limit based on changing circumstances and market conditions, but it's worthwhile to think about a starting point before you dive into investing. I'd recommend consulting a reputable financial adviser to come up with a reasonable goal for your returns.

to the business. Less cash means less value on the books. The idea here is that you purchase these stocks "cheap" and watch them grow to become more valuable.

Look for Value

With a value investing strategy, the investor looks to invest in companies that are "beaten-down" and undervalued. Understand and pay close attention to businesses that have been hit by short-term struggles. Ask yourself if the company can overcome the problem. If you think they can (and the research supports this), then you may be able to take advantage of lower share prices. For example,

Research in Motion (makers of the BlackBerry) was having patent problems just a few years ago. If you invested in RIM at that time, you would have saved 20 to 30 per cent on their share price. Another good example might be a clothing outfitter facing a huge increase in demand. If they don't have enough inventory on hand to meet the initial orders, their share price might drop in value. If they can overcome this short-term inventory struggle, they can and will experience growth. If you choose to try your hand at this strategy, ensure that you do your research. Newspapers, magazines, and online financial sites can be wonderful sources of information.

INVEST IN WHAT YOU KNOW

Peter Lynch is a famous investor that uses the buy-and-hold strategy that was described in the Long Haul section on page 129. Another key to his success is his "invest in what you know" approach. With this strategy, you simply invest in companies that you know a lot about. For example, a young professional might invest in Sony or Honda or Le Château. All of these companies are visibly recognizable. As well, doing research on things that interest you is never difficult or boring!

8
Get Specific:
HOMES, KIDS, AND STUFF LIKE THAT

This chapter deals with specific situations that may or may not apply to you right now. However, at some point in your life, these things (education, house-hunting, retirement, even children) may be very relevant. For example, if you are sixteen and in high school, you might not be thinking about kids or houses just yet. However, if you are nearing the end of your university degree, you might be considering purchasing a home in the near future. If you are married or engaged and thinking about children, you might be interested in saving for your children's education. Regardless, one thing remains true: everyone—regardless of life situation—should be thinking about their financial future and retirement.

Education

Marla wants to go to university to become a teacher. She is aware that her education costs will be somewhere between $7,000 and $10,000 per year. Unfortunately, her parents are *not in a position to help her out. Although Marla has heard horror stories about student loans, she's beginning to wonder if they might be the only answer to her dilemma.*

Most investment books don't include strategies designed to help pay for education—but then again, most investment books aren't written for people under thirty! But what if, like Marla, you're facing the challenge of paying for your own education? You are not alone. Only a handful of people are lucky enough to go to school debt-free. Most students rely on lines of credit or student loans to get through. The average Canadian student graduates with about $20,000 in debt.

If you know in advance that you will have to pay for your own education, you might want to consider a **stacked** GIC strategy. Back in chapter 7, we learned that GICs are guaranteed investment certificates. Whatever you invest is guaranteed to stay safe and earn at least some interest while it is invested for a specified period of time. Most importantly, GICs have different maturity dates. So, you could invest in a GIC and have it mature anywhere from one to ten years from now. A stacked GIC strategy is sort of like a forced savings plan. It involves investing in GICs both before going to school and throughout school. With proper planning, you can ensure that one GIC will mature every year or semester throughout your post-secondary school career—effectively releasing a handy sum of money that will assist you in paying for tuition and books.

Let's use Marla, from the case study above, to show us how this can work. In the summer between grades ten and eleven, Marla gets a part-time job, maybe at a golf course. Since she's working full time throughout July and August, she manages to make about $3,000. Because she's still living at home with her mom and dad—who pay the mortgage, the bills, and for all of her food—Marla manages to save $2,000 from her earnings. At the end of the summer, she visits the bank, speaks to an adviser, and purchases a GIC with a decent rate of return and a two-year term, meaning that it will mature during her first year of post-secondary education.

The following summer, between grades eleven and twelve, Marla works at the same job and saves another $2,000. Once again, she visits the bank at the end of August, and purchases another two-year GIC with a decent rate of return. This means that, when she's about to start her second year of post-secondary school, her second GIC will be maturing.

See? If Marla continued with this pattern of saving and investing in a GIC every summer, she'd end up "stacking" her GICs (see the chart below) so that they matured at the beginning of each year of post-secondary school. I know, I know! First-hand experience has certainly taught me that $2,000 isn't enough to pay for a full year of post-secondary education, but it is $2,000 more than you'd have if you didn't invest, and it certainly puts a dent into those tuition costs!

YEAR 1 (GR. 10)	YEAR 2 (GR. 11)	YEAR 3 (GR. 12)	YEAR 4 (1ST YR.)	YEAR 5 (2ND YR.)	YEAR 6 (3RD YR.)	YEAR 7 (4TH YR.)
$2,000 invested at 4%		$2,163.20				
	$2,000 invested at 4%		$2,163.20			
		$2,000 invested at 4%		$2,163.20		
			$2,000 invested at 4%		$2,163.20	
				$2,000 invested at 4%		$2,163.20

New Dollars Invested
Maturity Value

Another thing to note: When Marla starts university or college, she can take advantage of the fact that she has an extra two months to work each summer. She can earn more, save more, and purchase more valuable GICs. A good deal all around!

Home, Sweet Home

Krista is a twenty-one-year-old student in her first year of university. She wants to move out of her suburban family home as soon as she is done her post-secondary education. She is currently paying for her tuition and books, and is wondering how she is going to afford a down payment. She has her heart set on a condo nearer to the city centre—close to her friends and potential employment opportunities.

Interestingly, the condo market has exploded in Canada over the past twenty years. Developers are targeting almost every demographic group, although "under thirties" seem to be the focus of much condo advertising. Why? Condos are typically less expensive than detached homes. They can be easily cared for and managed. They offer young people a perfect way to enter the market without being completely strapped for cash.

First-time home buyers face significant challenges when they enter the real estate market. Not only do they need to come up with a down payment in order to own, but homes—whether they are townhouses, condos, or houses—come with a **mortgage** attached. A mortgage is a long-term debt instrument used to pay for your home. It is like having a contract stating that a certain property, your home, will be pledged as security against the value of

THE COSTS AND VALUE OF EDUCATION

Have you ever wondered how much it costs you to go to school? The total cost for a four-year undergraduate degree is approximately $32,000—and this doesn't include living expenses or purchasing a computer and software! But it doesn't end there. Because you are in school, you give up the opportunity to work full time and make some money. Let's say you could count on an annual salary of $30,000. Over the course of your four-year degree, you'd be "losing" a potential $120,000. Add that to the $32,000 you're spending on tuition and books, and your post-secondary education is "costing" you $152,000!

Are you asking yourself why you should bother? The answer is that over the course of your lifetime, you will make at least *double* the income of someone without a post-secondary education. Your career choices (remember chapter 1? Choice equals freedom.) will be better and more varied, and your income greater. It's worth noting that when we refer to post-secondary education, we're not talking exclusively about colleges and universities. Throughout North America, there is a huge demand for trades. Students pursuing this path have to go through extensive apprenticeship programs, courses, and testing. Post-secondary education is no longer limited to degrees. Certificates, apprenticeships, working terms, and other options are also included.

the loan. So, if you don't make your payments, the bank will take your house. Oftentimes, mortgages take twenty to thirty years to pay off. This may sound scary, but a mortgage is, in fact, very beneficial in the long run. Home owners are at least *seventy times* wealthier than people who rent for their entire lives. Purchasing a home is one of the best long-term investments you can make.

So, how do you go about it? Well, you could start socking away money for that down payment in your chequing account, or hide your cash in a safety deposit box until you are ready to make the purchase. But you know at this point that these approaches aren't going to get you very far. Sure, you might gain some interest over the years, but you might also dip into your savings from time to time. All in all, these are terrible ways to save your money for a long-term, big-ticket item.

Remember Krista from the case study above? Well, she is actually in pretty good shape. She has two things going for her: she knows what she wants, and she's willing to figure out a way to make it happen. Because she has some time on her side—three to five years in school—she'll want to ensure that she's earning interest on the money she invests, and she'll want to make sure that she can't touch that money (and accidentally ruin her long-term dreams because of one fabulous pair of shoes!). It wouldn't hurt, either, for Krista to look for ways that she can grow her down payment while in the savings process.

The very first thing Krista needs to do is visit her financial institution. Taking into account local laws, interest rates, and her personal financial situation, an adviser will be able to determine how much money she needs to save to cover a down payment. The typical minimum down payment can be as little as 5 per cent of the value of the home. So if the home you are interested in costs $175,000, a 5 per cent down payment would be approximately $8,750.

In Krista's scenario, let's assume that she takes either three, four, or five years to save her money. Let's also assume that she is choosing to save from 5 to 25 per cent of the value of the home. Have a look at the table below to find out how much money she will have to save every month without accrued interest.

KRISTA'S SAVINGS PER MONTH	5% DOWN $8,750	10% DOWN $17,500	15% DOWN $26,250	20% DOWN $35,000	25% DOWN $43,750
3 Years (36 months)	$243.06	$486.11	$729.17	$972.22	$1,215.28
4 Years (48 months)	$182.29	$364.58	$546.88	$729.17	$911.46
5 Years (60 months)	$145.83	$291.67	$437.50	$583.33	$729.17

But what if Krista starts saving her money in a high interest savings account with compound interest or in a GIC with compound interest? Both of those investments are very safe and secure so that Krista won't have to worry about putting her down payment at risk. And she'll likely fetch a return rate of 2 to 4 per cent compounded annually, which would help her to reach her savings goal sooner than she expected. Let's assume that Krista decides to save for a 10 per cent down payment of $17,500 over the course of three, four, or five years with an investment rate of 3 per cent.

Over three years:

YEARS	SAVED PER YEAR	MONTHLY SAVINGS 10% DOWNPAYMENT	TOTAL SAVED	SAVED WITH INTEREST	SAVINGS INTEREST RATE
1	$5,833.32	$486.11	$5,833.32	$6,008.32	3%
2	$5,833.32	$486.11	$11,666.64	$12,196.89	3%
3	$5,833.32	$486.11	$17,499.96	$18,571.12	3%

Over four years (and with lower monthly savings):

YEARS	SAVED PER YEAR	MONTHLY SAVINGS 10% DOWNPAYMENT	TOTAL SAVED	SAVED WITH INTEREST	SAVINGS INTEREST RATE
1	$4,374.96	$364.58	$4,374.96	$4,506.21	3%
2	$4,374.96	$364.58	$8,749.92	$9,147.60	3%
3	$4,374.96	$364.58	$13,124.88	$13,928.24	3%
4	$4,374.96	$364.58	$17,499.84	$18,852.30	3%

Over five years (and with lower monthly savings):

YEARS	SAVED PER YEAR	MONTHLY SAVINGS 10% DOWNPAYMENT	TOTAL SAVED	SAVED WITH INTEREST	SAVINGS INTEREST RATE
1	$3,500.04	$291.67	$3,500.04	$3,605.04	3%
2	$3,500.04	$291.67	$7,000.08	$7,318.23	3%
3	$3,500.04	$291.67	$10,500.12	$11,142.82	3%
4	$3,500.04	$291.67	$14,000.16	$15,082.15	3%
5	$3,500.04	$291.67	$17,500.20	$19,139.65	3%

As you can see, time really is on Krista's side. With a little forethought and planning, she should have no trouble making her dream a reality!

Getting Aggressive: The Possibility of Leveraging

If you are fortunate enough to have saved a solid down payment for your home, and have already found your dream home, you should take a very aggressive approach to your next house-buying step: mortgage-rate shopping.

As with any other purchase, you want to be very certain that you are getting the best value for your dollar. When it comes to mortgage rates, even 0.5 per cent can make a huge difference in your monthly mortgage payments.

Monthly Mortgage Payment with a Twenty-five-year Amortization

Rate	100,000 (monthly payment)	150,000 (monthly payment)	200,000 (monthly payment)	250,000 (monthly payment)	300,000 (monthly payment)
5.0%	$582	$872	$1,163	$1,454	$1,745
5.5%	$610	$916	$1,221	$1,526	$1,831
6.0%	$640	$960	$1,280	$1,600	$1,919
6.5%	$670	$1,005	$1,340	$1,675	$2,009
7.0%	$700	$1,051	$1,401	$1,751	$2,101
7.5%	$732	$1,097	$1,463	$1,829	$2,195
8.0%	$763	$1,145	$1,526	$1,908	$2,290
8.5%	$795	$1,193	$1,591	$1,988	$2,386

It is also important to consider the power of leveraging (see chapter 7) when you're about to purchase a home. Paul has been very lucky. Thanks to a sizable donation from his grandmother, and some hard work at jobs both during the summer and throughout the school year, Paul has managed to save $60,000 toward a down payment. The condominium he's set his sights on costs $120,000. The bank has already told Paul that he only needs to put down 5 per cent, or $6,000, in order to secure the unit he wants. However, Paul is thinking seriously about using the entire $60,000.

Before he makes any hard and fast decisions, Paul should take a good look at the interest rate the bank is offering. If it's a good rate (fairly low), he might want to consider making his down payment as small as possible. Using this strategy, Paul would put down a small amount on his home, invest the much larger portion of his cash, and let the interest from his investments compound and grow.

Let's crunch some numbers and see how this works. Remember, Paul has saved $60,000, the condo costs $120,000, and the bank is only asking for a 5 per cent down payment, or $6,000. If he only put $6,000 down, he would be left with a mortgage of $114,000, and $54,000 to invest elsewhere (for simplicity's sake, we're going to leave real estate and financing fees out of the equation here).

Let's say that Paul finds an investment portfolio that is expected to return 8 per cent annually. Remember the future value of money formula (see chapter 7): $P \times (1 + i)^n$ (P is principal invested; i is interest rate; n is investment period). In Paul's case, the formula works out like this:

$$\$54,000 \times (1 + 0.08)^1 = \$58,320$$

What this means is that Paul can invest his $54,000 into that investment vehicle and in one year's time he will have earned $4,320 in return ($58,320–$54,000). He can now use that $4,320 to help pay off his mortgage or he could compound it back into his investment and grow his money even more.

And what's the flip side of the coin? What would have happened if Paul put the remaining $54,000 into his down payment? If Paul can take advantage of a low interest rate on his mortgage—one that is lower than what he is making on his investments (8 per cent), he will come out on top. For example, if he's paying 5.5 per cent on his mortgage and making 8 per cent on his investment portfolio, then theoretically he is ahead by 2.5 per cent (8 − 5.5 = 2.5). If the markets are performing quite poorly, he might end up making less than 8 per cent on his portfolio in the short run. If his rate of return on his investment portfolio was 4 per cent and his mortgage rate remains at 5.5 per cent, he is paying a greater amount of interest on his mortgage. Therefore, it is in his best interest to place additional money on the mortgage. There are a number of factors that play into this scenario. For example, the value of homes in certain areas increases substantially over time.

Registered Plans: Kids and Retirement

Registered plans are great investment vehicles for long-term, big-ticket items—things like a child's education or your own retirement. And if you think this stuff sounds way too far off to be worried about, remember chapter 1. If you don't care about and invest in your own future, who will? Waiting to win the lottery or inherit the family fortune is not a viable financial plan! And don't forget: the earlier you start, the better off you'll be.

The two most common registered plans are Registered Retirement Savings Plans (RRSPs) and Registered

Education Savings Plans (RESPs). It's helpful to think of a registered plan as a type of house—a house that needs to be decorated! An investor can fill that house with the types of "decorations" (investments) that he or she wants—mutual funds, stocks, index funds, and more (see chapter 7). As with any real house, the decorations are chosen according to the tastes and needs of the owner. Some people like flashy things; others go for classic style; others still might prefer a mix. Whatever your taste, a registered plan allows you to create a balanced portfolio that suits your needs and investment style.

RRSPs

Why bother with a registered plan? Why not just invest in each component separately? Good question. The answer lies back with that investment strategy I outlined in chapter 7—the one about always taking free money. When you set up and invest in an RRSP, you are saving for your retirement. The government of Canada appreciates this, and rewards your efforts by making the dollars that you invest in the RRSP tax deductible.

When you start an RRSP, you have the opportunity to invest up to 18 per cent of your annual income or to a maximum of the following:

YEAR	CONTRIBUTION LIMIT
2005	$16,500
2006	$18,000
2007	$19,000
2008	$20,000
2009	$21,000
2010	$22,000

Below is an example of someone with an income of $32,000, taxed at a rate of 26 per cent. If this person contributed $3,000 to his RRSP, he would get a taxable benefit of approximately $832.

	NO CONTRIBUTION	CONTRIBUTION OF $3,000
Income	$32,000	$32,000
Tax Rate	26%	26%
Taxes Paid	$8,320	$7,488
RRSP Contribution	$0	$3,000
Deferred Tax	$0	$832

Now don't go getting all excited! This doesn't mean that you never pay taxes on the amount that you invest. When you do actually retire, and you start cashing in your investments so that you can continue to pay your bills and buy food and take vacations, you will pay taxes on whatever you withdraw.

So when should you start investing? Is it ever really too early to start thinking about retirement? Not really. Typically, people start investing in RRSPs when they get their first full-time job. The easiest set up for an RRSP is to time your contributions with your paycheques. So, if you get paid once per month, ensure that you contribute to your RRSP on that day. Similarly, if you get paid biweekly, set your contributions to match those days. RRSPs can be set up with as little as $25 a month. As your income and lifestyle changes, adjust your contributions accordingly. Here are some RRSP tips:

- Increase the size of your contribution when you get a raise. When you get a raise, you end up paying more in taxes. An increased RRSP contribution will help you save on your taxes.

- Match your risk level in your RRSP with your comfort level and your lifestyle. For example, if you have a child, you might want to consider placing some of your money in safer investments for security reasons.
- Maximize the benefits of any RRSP work plans. Usually employers will help fund your RRSPs. Take advantage of free money.

BORROWING TO INVEST?

An RRSP loan can be a wonderful thing. This type of loan is designed for people without available savings that want to make an RRSP contribution before the end of February so that its taxable benefit counts for the previous taxable year. For example, to get a taxable benefit for 2005, I would have to make an RRSP contribution before the end of February 2006. Oftentimes, this type of loan has a very reasonable interest rate attached and can be paid off within a year or two. The only reason someone should take out the RRSP loan is if the taxable benefit they receive from their RRSP contribution is greater than the amount of interest they will pay on the loan. The majority of the time, this does make sense. I'd recommend bargaining for the best interest rate possible and ensuring that you can indeed afford to make the monthly payments.

RESPs

A Registered Education Savings Plan is a long-term vehicle that a parent, grandparent, or legal guardian can establish for a child's post-secondary education. The only thing that is needed for this type of investment is a social insurance number for the child. As with an RRSP, the contributor fills the "house" with the types of investments that suit the investor. Also like an RRSP, the government is willing to help: the government contribution (the Canadian Education Savings Grant) will match 20 per cent of your contributions up to a total of $800 a year. Contributions can be made up until the child reaches the age of sixteen. In the table below, the assumption is made that the child attends post-secondary school at the age of eighteen. As you can see, the extra savings that the government contributes can be exceptionally valuable in the long run.

Although there is no tax credit for your contribution, there is one for the government's, and it is 20 per cent on the first $4,000 contributed each year. So, basically, the child gets the credit instead in the form of free money.

If your child decides not to go to school, the money you've invested and the interest it has earned still belongs to you. The government money (and its interest), is taken back.

CHILD'S AGE	YOUR $'S SAVED PER MONTH	YOUR $'S SAVED PER YEAR	GOVERNMENT CONTRIBUTION (20% OF YOUR CONT.)	VALUE OF THE RESP	RATE OF RETURN
1	100	1,200	240	1,555.20	8.0%
2	100	1,200	240	3,234.82	8.0%
3	100	1,200	240	5,048.80	8.0%
4	100	1,200	240	7,007.91	8.0%
5	100	1,200	240	9,123.74	8.0%
6	100	1,200	240	11,408.84	8.0%
7	100	1,200	240	13,876.74	8.0%
8	100	1,200	240	16,542.08	8.0%
9	100	1,200	240	19,420.65	8.0%
10	100	1,200	240	22,529.50	8.0%
11	100	1,200	240	25,887.06	8.0%
12	100	1,200	240	29,513.23	8.0%
13	100	1,200	240	33,429.49	8.0%
14	100	1,200	240	37,659.04	8.0%
15	100	1,200	240	42,226.97	8.0%
16	100	1,200	240	47,160.32	8.0%
17	0	0	0	50,933.15	8.0%
18	0	0	0	55,007.80	8.0%

Conclusion

You've embarked on a wonderful journey—a journey to better your financial knowledge. You now know more about investments and basic finance, and the tools that will help you achieve your financial dreams, than you did when you picked up this book. You are well equipped to become rich by thirty!

Still, you may find yourself wondering where you go from here. You aren't alone. It's completely normal to be overwhelmed by so much information. So, if you find your head spinning, or if you're worried about losing your focus, concentrate on the following ten pieces of advice. They'll ensure that you stay the course.

Ten Pieces of Advice

1. **Start now.** Whatever your financial situation may be, start to invest right now. Time is of the essence. The longer you wait, the less wealthy you'll become.

Think of it like this: by waiting, you are actually cheating yourself out of money. Start investing when you are young. You'll thank yourself later on.

2. **Take control.** Healthy money management requires that you learn to spend wisely, handle debt appropriately, and sometimes change your priorities. Use tools like realistic budgeting and planning to help you achieve your financial goals.

3. **If you don't need it, don't buy it!** Overspending can have an incredibly negative influence on your life. Couples that have spending problems, for example, are typically the first in line for a divorce! Overspending can spiral into debt and bankruptcy—and that affects every area of your life. You can control your spending! It just requires a change in your mindset.

4. **It doesn't matter what you have, it's what you do with it that counts.** You could be the poorest person on the block. You might only have $25 to save each month. You might only have $10! It doesn't matter. Do it! Don't be discouraged. There are thousands of very wealthy people who are wealthy now that started with almost nothing. You can do it, too!

5. **Try mutual funds.** If you're looking for a relatively safe and easy way to maximize your return—even with a very small initial investment—mutual funds are the way to go. They allow you to get into the market, to diversify, and to contribute limited funds.

6. **Contribute regularly.** By contributing to your investment portfolio regularly, you get to take advantage of the average price over the long haul. You don't have

to worry about timing the market. Leave that to the experts.

7. **Diversify!** If you have all of your eggs in one basket, and you drop that basket, all of your eggs are going to break. Diversify your investments to reduce your risks.

8. **Be patient.** Money grows exponentially over the long run. It doesn't necessarily grow immediately. Hang on for the ride. Markets change so much through time. They go up and they go down. Try to see past the short-term fluctuations and focus on the long term. In the long term, the markets will perform with a return of 11 to 13 per cent. Investors that focus on the short term tend only to make about 4 per cent. Figure out a strategy that suits your risk tolerance level, and stick with it through thick and thin.

9. **Pay yourself first.** You need to balance your debt reduction with saving and investing. Don't concentrate on one area and ignore the other. Use the "debt reduction" technique outlined in chapter 4 to get rid of the debt that's holding you back, but always ensure that you are saving some money as well. Saving for your future should be the top priority on your personal budget.

10. **Strike a balance.** Don't forget the three principles of wealth: spend wisely, save and invest, and give back to your community. This last item can be achieved by volunteering, or by donating funds or goods to a charity. You'll feel good knowing that you've done something positive for the community and for yourself.

You can refer back to these pages whenever you need a refresher course, or just a little motivation. I also recommend that you further enrich your knowledge of money management by continuing to learn and practice healthy money management techniques. Check out my website, www.richbythirty.com for my personal newsletter, an excellent glossary of terms, and some good links to other financial sites.

Now get out there and get going!

Index

Italicized numerals indicate charts, graphs, spreadsheets, etc.

advertising, 65–66, 139
aggressive growth funds,
118, 123
    sample portfolio,
    122–23, *122*
American Express, 71
assets, 51
ATB Financial (Alberta
Treasury Branch), 36
automated banking serv-
ices, 83–84, 97 (*See also*
online banking)

baby boomers, 21
balance, 89, 97, 118,
121–26, 154 (*See also*
diversification)
balanced growth portfo-
lios, 124–25, *125*
bank accounts
    checking accounts,
    37–38

checklist, 39–40
savings accounts, 38
setting up, 36–37
bank cards, 38–39
bank statements, 32
bankruptcy, 47, 56, 153
banks
    choosing, 37
    and customer service,
    41–42
    list of, 36
    online services, 34
    relationship with,
    35–36
    (*See also* online bank-
    ing; personal banker;
    telephone banking)
bargain hunting, 78–79
bear market, 107
big-ticket purchases,
33–34
    and investment vehi-
    cle, 116–117
    and leveraging,
    131–32
    and market cycle, 106

and registered plans,
146
researching, 65–66
biweekly payments, 70,
71, 73–75
BlackBerry, 135
BMO Bank of Montreal,
36
bonds, 109, 113–16
    rate of return, 115
    rating, *115–16*
brokerage accounts, 41
budgets
    and deficit, 50–51,
    53–61
    defined, 44–45
    and surplus, 50–53
budgets—creating
    assets & liabilities,
    51
    blending income with
    expenses, 49–50
    calculating net income
    or loss, 50–51
    and debt reduction
    strategy, 70

expenses, 47–50
income, 46, 49–50
bulk buying, 80
bull market, 107
business cycle. *See* market
cycles
buy-and-hold strategy,
129–30, 135

Caisse Populaire, 36
Canada Deposit
Insurance Corporation
(CDIC), 111
Canada Pension Plan
(CPP), 21
Canada Revenue Agency,
51
Canadian Education
Savings Grant, 150
cars
payments, biweekly, 74
purchasing, 65–66
cash flow, 54–55, 71, 100
charitable donations, 154
checking accounts, 37–38
choice, 21–23, 71, 140
CIBC, 36
commission, working on,
100
compound interest,
24–25, *25*, 91, 93–96
and bonds, 115
power of, *94–95*
computer programs,
spreadsheets, 33–34
condo market, 139
consolidation loan,
73
consumer spending,
63–64
contraction (market
cycle), 106
corporate bonds,
114–15
corporations
assessing financial
health of, 112

and dividend
signalling, 130–31
and value investing,
134–35
cover letter, résumé, 43
credit cards, 40
benefits of, 68
and frugal life strategy,
79
interest on, 67–68, 70,
79
minimum payments,
70–71
organizing bills, 32
credit rating, 68
credit unions, 36
customer service, 41–42

debit cards, 38–39
debt reduction
schedule, *72*
strategies, 69–75
debt-to-equity ratio,
112
debts
biweekly payments,
70–71, 73–75
causes of, 64–65
consolidating, 73
corporate, 112
and extra payments,
70
highest-interest-bear-
ing, 70
identifying, 69–70
loans to pay off, 55
student loans, 137
deficit, 50–51, 53–61
dealing with, tips,
53–55
deposit-only saving
account, 83
deposits
automated, 83–84
minimum, bank
accounts, 37
disposable income, 63–64

diversification, 118,
120–26, 154 (*See also*
balance)
dividends
defined, 111
investment strategy,
130–31
documents, organizing,
32–33
dollar cost averaging,
126–27
Dow Jones, 120
Dogs of the Dow
Strategy, 133–34
down payments, 53, 76,
139
minimum, 141–42
saving for, *142, 143*

eBay, 43, 61
education
cost/value of, 140
registered plan. *See*
RESPS
tuition fees, 23, 68,
136–39
electronic (bank) trans-
fers. *See* automated
banking services
emergencies
credit card and, 68
fund, 55, 89
employer-sponsored
retirement savings plans,
127–28, 149
entertainment, 80
entrepreneurship, 43
Excel, 33
exchange-traded funds.
See index funds
expansion (market cycle),
105–6
expenses
categories, 48
tracking, 35, 47–50

fast food, 80

fees
    checking accounts,
        37–38
    mutual funds, 119
    savings accounts, 38
    stocks, 112
    (*See also* service fees)
file folders, 32–33
file names, 32–33
financial advisers, 42
financial pages, 35,
    104–105, 112
food habits, 80–81
freedom, 23, 71, 140
free money. *See* employer-
    sponsored retirement
    savings plans
frugal life, tips, 78–82
    (*See also* lifestyle
    changes)
full-service brokers, 41
fun expenses, 48
future value formula,
    132–33, 145–46

GICs (Guaranteed
    Investment Certificates),
    110, 117
    (*See also* stacked GICs)
goals
    action/dream para-
        digm, 26
    investment, 27–28,
        99–100, 125
    long-term, 27, 92
    realizing, tips, 26–27
    short-term, 27
    SMART, 27–28
    writing down, 27, 29,
        83
government bonds, 114
growth & balanced
    income investments,
    123
growth funds, 25, 91,
    118, 123

health plan, tax deduc-
    tions, 21
healthy lifestyle, 81
heating/electricity. *See*
    utilities
holiday spending, 54, 58
home maintenance, DIY,
    61
home poverty, 50, 56–61
home, purchasing, 139,
    141–43

income-producing fund,
    118
income tax, 51, 100
income, tracking, 35, 46,
    49–50
index funds, 110, 120–21
inflation, 20–21
ING Direct, 36
instant gratification,
    64–65, 67
interest
    on bonds, 113–14
    and checking
        accounts, 37
    on credit cards, 67,
        70, 79
    on initial investment,
        24 (*See also* com-
        pound interest)
    and savings accounts,
        38
interest rates
    credit cards, 67, 70
    and GICs, 117
    and market cycle, 106
    and mortgages, 75
    negotiating, 79
    and RRSP loan, 149
Interior Savings (bank),
    36
international funds, 118
Internet, 34, 36 (*See also*
    websites, financial)
investing
    benefits of, 92, *92*

commitment to,
    96–97
and compound inter-
    est, 93–96, *94–95*
emotional reaction to,
    129–30
information sources.
    See financial pages;
    online investment
    sites; websites
meaning of, 90–91
objectives of, 91–92
terminology, 105–7,
    123
tips, 97–98
and waiting, 152–53
investment
    automating services,
        39, 97
    and big-ticket pur-
        chases, 116–117
    goals, 27–28, 99, 100
    growth-oriented, 25
    interest on, 24 (*See
        also* compound inter-
        est)
    long-term. *See* bonds;
        home, purchasing;
        mutual funds
    lump-sum, 126
    and market cycles,
        105–7
    and money schedule,
        99–100
    and regular contribu-
        tions, 153–54 (*See
        also* dollar cost aver-
        aging)
    Rule of 72, 25
    self-managed, 120
    short-term. *See* T-bills
    statements, 33, 130
    and time horizon, 99
    tracking online, 34
investment options,
    108–9
    bonds, 109, 113–16

GICs, 110, 117
index funds, 110, 120–21
mutual funds, 110, 118–19
savings accounts, 109, 111
stocks, 109, 111–13
T-bills, 110, 116–17
investment strategy
buy-and-hold, 129–30, 135
buy low, sell high, 133–34
diversification & balance, 121–26, 154
dividend strategies, 130–31
dogs, 133–34
dollar cost averaging, 126–27
investing in what you know, 135
knowing your limits, 134
leveraging, 131–33
registered retirement savings, 127–29
value investing, 134–35
investor
involvement level of, 100
knowledge, 112, 121, 125–26, 135
moderate, 103
non-risky, 103
profile, 98–104
risk tolerance of, 100–4
risky, 104

jobs, 43

leveraging, 131–33, 144–46

liabilities, 51
lifestyle changes, 53–54, 60, 69 (*See also* frugal life; healthy lifestyle)
tips, 61
liquidity, 91
loans, 55
consolidation, 73
and leveraging, 131–32
RRSP, 149
student, 137
Lynch, Peter, 135

mandatory expenses, 48
market
cycles, 105–7
defined, 105
timing, 154
trends, 130, 131
marketing, 65–66
maturity dates
bonds, 114, 115
GICs, 117, 137
T-bills, 116
Monster, 43
mortgage(s)
defined, 139, 141
biweekly payments, 74
monthly payments, *144*
rates, 144
mutual fund managers, 119
mutual funds, 110, 118–19, 153
categories, 118
cost of, 118–19
defined, 118
management fees, 119
return rate, 107, 119, 129
and risk, 118

need vs. want, 76, 78–79
newspapers. *See* financial pages

New York Stock Exchange, 105

online
banking, 34–35, 39, 88 (*See also* automated banking services)
investment sites, 112
job search, 43
trading account, 41
organization process and banking, 35–42
file folders, 32–33
spreadsheets, 33–34
and timing, 34–35
overspending, 35, 39, 153. *See also* debt; deficit

patience, 154
paying yourself first, 81, 83–84, 154
peak (market cycle), 106
personal banker, 37, 40, 42
personal net worth, 51
portfolio, defined, 105
portfolio manager, 118
portfolios—samples
aggressive growth, 122–23, *122*
balanced growth, 124–25, *125*
conservative growth, 123–24, *124*
President's Choice Banking (PC), 40–41
President's Choice Financial, 36

RBC Royal Bank, 36, 40–41
real estate market, 139, 141–46
recession (market cycle), 106

recovery (market cycle), 106

registered plans. *See* RESPS; RRSPS

Research in Motion, 135

RESPs (Registered Education Savings Plans), 128, 146–47, 150, *151*

résumés, 43
    retirement savings plans, 127–28 (*See also* registered plans)

rewards, 52

risk
    level, and corporation, 112
    and mutual funds, 118
    and reward, 115
    and RRSPs, 149
    tolerance, 100–4

RRSPs (Registered Retirement Savings Plans), 128, 146, 147–49
    contribution limit, *147*
    loan, 149
    tax benefits, 148, *148*
    tips, 148–49

Rule of 72, 25–26

savings accounts, 25, 38, 83, 92, *92*, 109, 111

savings formula, monthly, 86–87

savings plan, 82–84, 88

Scotia Bank, 36

secondary expenses, 48

sector funds, 120–21

service fees, 40–42

shareholder, 111

SMART goals, 27–28

S&P 500 (Standard & Poor's), 113, 120

spending habits, 54–55

spreadsheets
    budgeting, 46–49, 56–60
    computer program, 33–34
    investment progress, 97–98

stacked GIC, 137–38, *138*

stock market, 100, 104–105
    losing money on, 112–113
    rate of return, 107, 113, 129

stocks, 109, 111–13
    vs. bonds, 114–15

surplus, 50–51, 53

tax
    deductions, 21
    minimization, 91,

100, 128, 147, 148–49
    return, 51

T-bills (Treasury bills), 110, 116–17

TD Canada, 36

Technology Bubble, 131

telephone banking, 39

Toronto Stock Exchange, 105

trading accounts, 41

trough (market cycle), 106

under-spending. *See* surplus

utilities, 32, 61

vacations, 52, 54–55, 76–77

value investing, 134–35

VanCity Bank (Vancouver), 36

VISA, 70–71

vision statement, 28–29, 85

volunteerism, 154

websites, financial, 34–36, 155

Workopolis, 43

youth market, 63–64